GOD

— the —

GREAT PLANNER

The Journey Home Daughter

LORAINE *and* JOHN GIBSON

authorHOUSE®

AuthorHouse™ UK
1663 Liberty Drive
Bloomington, IN 47403 USA
www.authorhouse.co.uk
Phone: 0800.197.4150

Scripture quotations marked NKJV are taken from the New King James Version.
Copyright © *1982 by Thomas Nelson, Inc. Used by permission. All rights reserved.*

Published by AuthorHouse 03/29/2016

ISBN: 978-1-5246-3004-1 (sc)
ISBN: 978-1-5246-3002-7 (hc)
ISBN: 978-1-5246-3003-4 (e)

Print information available on the last page.

This book is printed on acid-free paper.

TO
David and Ruth Parkinson
&
Jill Holt

For Being There

Thank you

I would like to say thank you to the Nursing Times for their kind permission to reproduce three articles that was written by Loraine Gibson as she was going through the bone marrow transplant these articles remain the copyright of the Nursing Times magazine.

- ➤ Chronis Meyloid Leukemia (Published June 8, 1983)
- ➤ Bone Marrow Transplant – Process (Published January 21, 1987)
- ➤ Bone Marrow Transplant – Recovery (Published January 28, 1987)

FOREWORD

I thought I would write a brief letter to accompany my testimony. The testimony was written many years ago and is only a section of the amazing events and actions that God in His Grace has done for me. It was written many years ago and was written as a young naïve Christian. I could have rewritten the testimony in retrospect and corrected the immature beliefs that I had when I wrote it originally but I wanted to you to read it as it was written then in 1983. There are many inconsistencies regarding my Faith and opinions which have changed over the years as I matured in my walk with God and I hope that I have demonstrated that God will guide you and is patient with at least with one young believer and will guide you also through Jesus and the Holy Spirit so persevere until the end and read this letter as well.

During the years to date I hope to share with you and demonstrate that verse in 1 Peter 'that whatever matters to me matters to Him. How awesome is that, the Creator of the Universe, cares about me. He has used situations to teach me obedience, trust, faith and patience. God has a Plan for me and He asks only two things ~I listen and obey no matter how strange it seems in human terms.

I hope that my testimony encourages you to Trust where God leads you and to believe that He has such power and ability to help you on your journey. Even if you cannot see where it lead's. You may be helped by the unexpected and the most unlikely circumstances or people. How every seemingly insignificant action or moment is not an accident but by God's Will and Plan.

Oh he won't do anything for me is often the cry I hear I am too insignificant. You are a son or daughter of a royal priesthood. I have been through many serious situations I have survived meningitis, had Leukaemia, illnesses, been critically ill twice, been sacked twice relating to being a Christian, my home and finances taken away from me, my reputation and the list goes on but wait I have been Blessed so much as all the situations were managed by God, this is one of the inconsistencies. In my early walk with God I believed He gave all this woe to me to teach me to help others, be stronger, trust Him more but this is not so... Satan does this to you, God uses these situations according to His Plan and Will. Jesus paid the price for you to be free. You will be supported by Almighty God whew that is awesome.

A minister once said to me nothing improves Prayer time and Trust than big trouble. I had to search and pray and listen so I could trust Him especially when I had cancer. I had to take such a leap of Faith and obey what God was saying to me, stop all your medication, don't listen to the consultants when they said you will die or you won't need the treatment. I had to learn to Trust and lean not on what I understood but God's wisdom, not see through human eyes but see through the eyes of faith; make no mistake it is not so easy as you think especially when your life is in the balance.

Situations have occurred and I have not listened and been disobedient but God so loves us He is ready to forgive us if we turn to Him and ask His forgiveness and He has been there to guide me through the consequences of my disobedience. Be not afraid...

I am very Blessed and helped may people through my experiences and I hope that reading this testimony that you too will be blessed, strengthened and encouraged. This isn't the testimony of a mighty minister or a powerful evangelist but is the true account of how God worked His Will on ordinary person just like you who has done wonderful and amazing things in the life of an ordinary down to earth person and is continuing to do so.

Loraine Gibson   The Mouse

CHAPTER ONE

Time out to think.

1983

Many people believe that God exists in some vague manner and that He also influences their lives in some vague manner. Very few people stop and actually take time out to look back over their life and evaluate just how much God has been active and influenced their lives. People are just so busy in these times of rushing about trying to get things done that they do not take the time to think back and see what changes of direction that have occurred or opportunities that have arisen, this is true of some Christians too.

If you do not stop and find a peaceful haven and take time to meditate over changes how you will fully appreciate them. How can you judge whether you have wandered off from a goal that you set yourself if you don't take time or that you feel God may have set for you without the time for reflection and time out to see? I have much respect for the mature persons who would fast and reflect as part of a routine to help them to hear what God has asked of them; so often this is not a "trendy" aspect of modern Christian worship (as I write this in 1983)

In a busy world with fast changing ideals and values people have forgotten to take the time to reflect on their lives and their relationship with God. This is a common fault among Christians, so busy in the activities of their churches that they forget to be still long enough for the Lord to speak to them. Meditation and reflection need not take long, it can be done anywhere where it's quiet and where you won't have constant interruptions. All you need is some time and some peace and it could make a vast difference to your life. I will tell you how it changed mine.

I have taken some time and have reflected on my life and am amazed at just what the Lord has done for me. I am even more amazed when I see just how much planning has gone into my life right down to the seemingly insignificant details. Even as I write I am again at a crossroads and am waiting on the Lord to guide me. I must decide, with God's help, which direction I should go in now and I pray and await the answer. I believe God will as before, guide me into the right decision because I have had many crossroads in my life and I know that for every one of the directions I have taken It was through God's guidance; and just to put things in perspective I have made decisions that looking back were not of Gods plan but mine own endeavors ... see Christians can get it wrong if they don't listen....

I must look at my past and check that I have indeed stayed faithful to the advice that God gave me. I must check that I have trodden the path that the Lord showed me and you can't do that without taking time to look back. I must pray and show God what I have achieved and then wait for the most important part which is to wait for the word of the Lord.

I have written this testament to show you just how far God plans our lives and to show you that it happens to ordinary people like you and me. I have read many testaments from famous people and thought that this was a special person and that it wouldn't happen to me. How wrong I was and I will show you.

I am an ordinary person, I'm not a great Christian nor am I famous. It took me some time to learn that I am a special person to God, as you are. I believe that if you live like Christ, there are ups and downs. One aspect is that in each life that you touch, each kind deed that you do, even each good thought that you have will help someone somewhere. Each life that you touch no matter how briefly will give that person smothering special of Christ. It's like a domino effect, you help someone, and they help someone and so on. Think about that, isn't it mind blowing each life you touch will give someone something of Christ.

I in my turn want to help you. I want you to know about what God has done for me, I want you to know that God Plans my life and yours down to the last detail and want you to know that it happens to ordinary people like you and me,

My testament is not depressing but it is sad in places. It's full of the wonder that I feel for God and what he has done for me; you share with me my experiences as I look back and meditate and you take time to reflect on your own life. Follow the hopes and fears of an ordinary person and learn to Trust the Lord. Take courage and renew your faith from my words so that I can stand before the Lord and say I helped someone with the help and the guidance of my Father, God.

CHAPTER TWO

I meet my God

Once upon a time….. Well that's enough of that we'll scrap that bit perhaps. Once I was a young girl, yes once, with the usual aspirations of young girls. I wanted to fall in love and be happy. I wasn't very particular about who the boy should be he needn't be a prince but he should worship me and need me and love me very much. Not a lot to ask I'm sure you will agree!

As a young girl I had always felt close to God, I didn't understand why but I accepted it as so. I went to the local sunshine groups and enjoyed Sunday School and felt good about being a child of God.

I lived at home with my parents and I went through the usual teenage frustrations which makes me very ordinary doesn't it? I conformed more than some, being a bit timid and quiet. My favorite pastime was to shut myself up in my bedroom with a good book and just ignore everything around me Sounds familiar, does it?. I got all my idealistic views on love and marriage from romantic nove.ls where the heroine is saved from a fate worse than death, just in the nick of time by, the charming and handsome hero.

I didn't get on too well with my Mother and I was conscious, even at a young age of needing her approval and afraid to do anything in case I got her disapproval instead. She appeared to me to be a very unemotional person and I felt that she was constantly disapproving of me and that I could never match up to her high ideals; I was very naive and indecisive and this did not help me in the least.

I never made any big decisions on my own and really I lived a rather tepid kind of life this was soon to change as my first boyfriend arrived on the scene and began to stir up me and my life. I went from sitting in my little bedroom to wanted to go and I think that the changes were a bit sudden for my Mother. I was flung into a romantic whirlpool of emotions and I was really out of my depths. I was trying to cope with this intensity of feeling and the rather hostile reaction of my parents to this event. I met my boyfriend (John) only twice and then we decided to get married, I knew somehow that this was God, some instinctive feeling. I very out of character asked him to marry me on the second I occasion that I met him. He knew too that this was to be, he was a Catholic at this time, he had stood up with very young children and at the age of 13 years (and he was a very tall boy) to give his life to God. Big change isn't it from little Cinderella to a married woman. The quiet little mouse really changed not fully realizing at this stage that it was God working his Plan out in my life. and I began to live life for myself. I can hear you thinking that this will end in disaster but you will have to read on a find out what happens.

John was a bit old fashioned and he called at my home to introduce himself to my parents this didn't seem to go down too well. He braved my Mothers disapproving stare which could reduce me to blubbering jelly but he didn't bat an eyelid. He did accompany us on one or two family outings and I was allowed to see him. Soon though it became apparent that I was getting a little too serious and my parents decided to put a stop me seeing him. I can now understand their anxiety but could I see reason then, no chance. I became very determined that I would continue seeing him and this caused turmoil in the home. I was under a great deal pressure to stop seeing him and normally I would have given up long ago but this time I decided I wouldn't, You can see where the strong decisions in my life have been initiated by God as part of His Great Plan....

Emotionally I was being pulled apart, first my family then John. This continued on for some time and eventually I decided that I had enough so I left home. I left a note and packed my few belongings in a carrier bag, it was full of childish memories; I took a giant teddy bear that John had won for me at the funfair a few children's books I realize now that there must have been an easier way than this but I found my Parents difficult to talk to and I knew that I could eventually give in under the pressure.

I can still remember the pain that leaving caused me and did for many years after. I thought that I was strong and able to stand on my own two feet when in reality I had been cushioned against the ways of the world and I learnt the lessons the hard way. I expected my parents to forgive and forget after but it never worked out that way. I was very emotionally affected and it was a very traumatic time for me. I know it was hard on my parents now, but I could see no other way of doing it. When relationships between my parents and I remained strained I felt very neglected and hurt and pride refused to let me show just how this affected me. Are you affected yet? If not there's more to come.

I went to live with John and he coped well with my problems, nightmares, sleep walking and generally growing up. He stood beside me despite my turbulent emotions and I clung to him like a raft. He was a little more mature than I and he had grown up more aware of basic ideas of living than I ever had and he had learnt from his experiences during a very hard childhood. My relationship worsened with my family but each Christmas I determined that I would send a card to them and a little present. I considered their attitude to be very harsh. I really missed being part of the family and I missed my younger brother dreadfully I was always very withdrawn and upset at Christmas time.

I spent a year just drifting along slowly recovering from all the emotional turmoil. John was the only stable element in my life at this time or so I thought at the time. I had a feeling about God but I did not understand or stop to see how He was influencing my life.

My life was taking the usual course, young girl leaves home infatuated with boy, all the trappings of a soap opera really. True to this picture I then became pregnant and as I was living with John and his Mother this really set the cat amongst the pigeons. My mother was disgusted with me and told me I had ruined my life. John's Mother wasn't too impressed either and she rather resented me being in her home. She was a very hard woman, John and his sister were often the recipients of a battering and physical and mental abuse. The atmosphere became very strained and it seemed to me that even John seemed to be ignoring me. I went to see my local doctor and the first thing he offered me was an abortion. In view of my emotional state he persuaded me that it would be for the best and made me an appointment for the hospital to see a consultant.

I attended the hospital the following week; it was like a cattle market. I saw two different doctors and they gave me brief and vague details of what would happen to me. It was worded in such a way that I thought I was doing the right thing and I did not understand just what really was involved in an abortion. I was a very naïve person and I truly did not know about the killing of a life. I expected to go to sleep and when I woke up the baby would be gone. I remember walking home in the pouring rain my mind going over and over what had been said to me. I really believed that I would not manage if I had the baby and yet I wanted to keep it.

I walked round like that for ages, just walking about in the rain, going round in circles in my mind. I noticed a little church while I was walking and if it was open. I would go in. I was so desolate and so alone and when you get into such a state, you don't seem to be able to work anything out. I sat on the bench, outside just sobbing for ages. Eventually I went into the quietness of the church and was soothed by its stillness. I have always even from a young child knew that I was safe in a church and that God heard me and that I felt a special bond. I knelt and prayed, it came straight from my heart and my despair. This was the first time I had been in a church since I was about fourteen and had attended Sunday school. I didn't know how to pray but I just spoke out the things that I was feeling. I spoke of my fear and my pregnancy, I spoke of my family and how I felt, and it all just poured out. Suddenly a sense of peace invaded my mind and all my inner turmoil ceased instantly, a voice spoke to me, even then I didn't realize that it was the Lord that was speaking to me. The voice told me that my fears would leave me and that I should have the child and that I would be glad that I had in later years. The voice was quiet but with authority and it assured me that everything would be all right. I would never regret my decision to keep the baby.

This was my first understanding about the contact with God, it took some time to sink in but I walked away from that church calm and reassured. I would have the baby and I knew somehow that what the voice had said would happen and my fears disappeared. I little knew then just what this would mean to me later and how by asking the Lord into my life I had set a new direction in my life.

CHAPTER THREE

The Gift of Life

I was not immediately overwhelmed with God's love nor did I think my personality changed in some way. I was aware of a warm, toasty feeling, as I use to describe it. It was much later during some dramatic times that I became fully aware of Gods Influence in my life. I have read many testaments stating how the recipient was greatly changed overnight but with me it happened gradually over some years. My life was greatly changed in those years by the direct intervention of the Lord on many occasions.

Back to my pregnancy, when I told John that I had been to the hospital to see about an abortion he was furious. In these times we are often told, as women, that our bodies are our own and we should be able to choose what we wish to do with them. This is the excuse offered and a way to salve our conscious should we decide to have an abortion. Very little credence is given to the fathers' wishes and a recent court case was where the father wanted the girl to have the child and not to have an abortion and he would take responsibility of the child, He did not win his case and the girl had an abortion. John would have no say in the final decision according to law and public opinion about the baby, but needless to say I would have lost his love. I still had the form in my pocket that my Mother had to sign as I was only seventeen, to give her permission to have the baby aborted. She had signed it but she would never have forgiven me for it. Now all that had changed for I was to have the child. I told John about my talk with God and he accepted this without batting an eyelid. In his teens he himself had been told to be accepted into the catholic faith though there were no catholics in the family. He had stood with the little children and he stood five foot eight at this time and had been very embarrassed about it but he had obeyed the word of God.

We decided to be married as soon as possible and with this in mind I went to see my parents, Their attitude had not changed but there had been a rather startling development at home. My mother was now in her forties and when I went to visit her she was actually in bed with a two-day old baby, my new sister.

What a shock this was I had seen her two or three weeks earlier and she did not look pregnant. I thought life was strange but it wasn't till some eleven years later that I was to realize that this was the work of the Lord and just how he planned the details which often seems insignificant at the time and which would prove to be so vital.

I planned my wedding, it was a little difficult as I wasn't working and John was only on a small wage, The Lord provided for this and out of the blue we received a hundred-pound tax rebate which provided the material for the dresses and the flowers and even a car to take me to the church. A little drapery shop closed down in the town and provided me with little gloves and a veil and even the little silk flower headdresses for the bridesmaids. The only thing that I wish I could have afforded was a decent photographer as the only photographs I have are little snapshots which one of Johns family took. A friend of mine who lived next door to my mother helped me make my dress and when it was done I did show it to my mother. I hoped it would help clear the air but it didn't really work. The service was really nice the weather was good and my little lump didn't show. The only thing that marred the occasion was the fact that nobody from my side of the family came. I turned, to walk down the aisle and there was nobody sitting on my side of the church. I hoped that they would have a change of heart at the last minute, I had even sent them a beautiful wedding invitation but it was not to be. I was very hurt by this and though I have forgiven them occasionally I still remember that pain caused by their absence.

I settled down to married life; we got a council house two doors away from Johns Mother. I was beginning to enjoy being pregnant, I had lost my job when the management found out I was expecting; something that probably wouldn't happen today but we were managing on Johns wage. I saw more of my mother while I was pregnant and she gave me things that my sister no longer needed. It was really strange to visit and see this little baby in my mother's arms and I must admit to feelings of jealousy at times. My Mother was very good at this point and I began to hope things would now get back to an ordinary relattionship. Unfortunately, our relationship hasn't really improved so much but we see each other and now I have a family of my own.

The time came for my baby to be born. I has three false starts on a run I had false labour pains and it became a joke at the hospital. It always occurred on the day that it was roast dinner for lunch and was very good so this was blamed as the culprit. I began to get quite worried as the days went passed and it came to the week before Christmas. I tried the old remedies of castor oil and orange juice and hot baths but to no avail. Eventually I was taken in and the doctor decided, to break my waters ouch, that was very painful. I went into slow labour and by three thirty on Sunday I was struggling. I remember being very frightened and calling over and over for my Mum but it was always John holding my hand. As the pain got worse I became more confused and was taken into the delivery room. The nurse wouldn't let John in which was the practice of the day and I lay there so alone and scared, and the more frightened. I became the worse the pain was. Eventually my daughter was born with the aid of forceps and weighing in at eight pounds ten ounces oh the relief. I don't remember anything else except that my daughter required an incubator and needed special nursing for forty-eight hours. I didn't feel any strong maternal feelings for her when she was given to me after this time and this caused me some worry. I spent the next few days recovering and learning to care for this fragile bundle of life which thanks to the Lord I would be able to care for. I fed her myself and was so well endowed milk wise that I fed most of the babies in the maternity unit with my milk. I remember my husband John saying what a little cow I was which earned him a disapproving stare from a passing nurse and a quick kick on the shins from me.

Six days later and it was Christmas Eve and I was feeling very homesick and I cried so much that the doctor sent me home instead of keeping me in hospital for the full ten days. It was the first time that I had been separated from John and. I missed him terribly-- ah true love,

I arrived home rather suddenly and unexpectedly clutching my precious little bundle and because of the suddenness John didn't know that I was coming home. Unfortunately, he was a Part time fireman and he had been out all night on a fire and the ambulance men couldn't wake him up I had to go to his Mums until he could be woken up, what a homecoming that was. When he did surface at dinner time he was so pleased with his new daughter it made up for the waiting. To think that I nearly had an abortion and my daughter would never have existed and just been a statistic on a chart somewhere. Praise God ….

As my daughter was born so close to Christmas we called her Carol but the registrar tagged an 'e' onto the end so we ended up with Carole. She was a very good baby, very content and soon sleeping through the night. Her one little foible was that she had this knack of waking up when the film was on about seven o'clock and John would sit with her in his arms watching the film. He is a very good father and would do everything that I did including changing nappies and feeding, with a bottle of course....!!

Life went on in this pleasant way I was still insecure but I had settle down a lot by now we were very poor but happy. Our maim arguments were about money or the lack of it. I just had never learnt to budget and this caused us a lot of problems and even today I have no respect for money at all. I am not very materialistic at all and while this is considered a virtue it can cause a lot of problems.

CHAPTER FOUR

A Plan to save my Life

Three years passed where I was a Mother and a housekeeper. I'm not very good on the housework part. I understand the view of Quentin Crisp who thought dust was good and therefore never dusted. It is John who can clean and who cooks very well. The Lord certainly knew what he was doing when he paired us up together. I had every reason to be grateful of John's housekeeping skills later.

I began to think about having another child. Everyone advised me that I should wait another year or so before having another. I was too young to have another. I was much more stable emotionally and though it had been a hard struggle I felt that I would be able to manage if I had another child.

Financially things were a little sticky but this was nothing new and always, at the very last minute. Something would occur which would get me out of a sticky problem. I would only be twenty-two in a couple of years and this was still young for a child. Sounds very reasonable doesn't it? how wrong can you be. I sought the guidance of God and believed that I should try for a baby now, so I went ahead despite the overwhelming advice of everyone else not too. It often takes some time to conceive so I was expecting quite a wait. I have since worked out that I conceived on the day that I prayed and that was the very first day that it was possible to become pregnant. How great is God's planning and the power of prayer. The quickness of the conception is going to be very significant later as you will see.

I prayed for a son but I would be happy with whatever the Lord thought fit to give me. I had a very insignificant pregnancy but I must admit I enjoyed it more than my first as I was considerably more at peace with myself. Carole, my daughter, was told of the babies imminent arrival and didn't seemed bothered about the news. I was a little concerned about any jealousy that might have occurred but I didn't need to worry at all.

My baby was born one week late and nearly strangled himself with the cord. I was in hospital on my own when the baby was born as John had stayed at home to look after Carole. The birth went well and labour didn't need to be induced... I was more in control and this contributed to how well the birth went. The baby was placed in an incubator to help as there were respiratory problems and also because there was infection in the umbilical cord which was quite serious. The baby of course was.........a boy, there that's put you out of your misery. I had to go home without him till this infection had cleared up. It took two weeks and. I missed him dreadfully. Each day Carole would ask when her brother was coming home when he arrived home we called him John and I am pleased to say he was another good baby though not as placid as Carole. His personality began to show very early on in his life. Carole loved him from the start. She (s)mothered him and would change his nappy with me and she loved to bath him and feed him, She was very patient with him and would take hours to teach him things and play with him. I enjoyed these years when they grew up together.

Time passed quickly and Carole began school and then it was John's turn. I had looked after John at home and I am glad of the time I spent with him. I began to think about what I should be doing in my life I was only twenty four and had two children. I didn't want any more children, being quite happy with a boy and a girl, I had matured like a good wine (tee hee) and was now much more stable in my emotions, having the children had done a lot for me but I found it increasingly difficult to find employment. I did not seem equipped to do anything but I carried on looking.

Then in one week I was inundated from a number of sources about nursing. I did not at first take it very seriously but one night John and I began to discuss it, it followed the pattern which we had previously discussed meant that the Lord was guiding us. On many occasions when we had prayed for guidance things occurred just like this and we would do whatever was being shown, I was very sceptical about nursing because of my character. I was lacking self-confidence and had become very shy and withdrawn. We had become a much insulated family, having no social contacts and very little family contacts. The thought of interviews scared me silly and exams and even medicals left me in a cold sweat.. The idea of a career in nursing was daunting to say the least.. I had got very fat and complacent and felt quite content in my safe and environment at home. I even got the shopping down to one day so I wouldn't have to keep going out. I just couldn't believe that the Lord really wanted me to try to get into nursing.

The first step was to attend an interview; I remember the day very well. This was my first major interview. It was snowing a blizzard and I had to go over isolated hill roads and on a number of occasions the bus actually got stuck.

When I eventually got to my interview I was passed caring whether I did well or not. I was so cold. The interview was conducted by a large black gorilla type man; who asked me all sorts of odd questions and his attitude seemed to be that he didn't really approve of married women working which was odd because he was Director of Nursing and had hundreds of women training as nurses. I came away feeling that I had failed the interview and to top it all the little bus did get stuck in the snow and I had to wait some time all on my own on this bus to be rescued.

I was extremely surprised to receive a letter stating that I had passed my preliminary interview and could now proceed onto the next stage. The next stage was the entrance examination. I was convinced that I would fail it had been nearly ten years since I had been at school and I had never taken any exams. The night before the exam I spent hours praying for help, I expect God was amused at my rather serious petition. The day of the exam I was nearly late due to some unforeseen complication, I sat down with a minute to spare all flustered and out of breath. Luckily the exam had a large content of English Language which was my favourite subject. I gained confidence doing the English questions but when I turned the page and saw the logic questions I could have cried, There were rows of little boxes with some squiggles in and you had to put them in order of sequence. I couldn't see any pattern at all they just looked like pretty patterns. I did get the hang of them eventually but I was again convinced that I had failed.

Again I received a letter stating that I had passed the exam; I couldn't believe it I could now go on to the next stage and that was interview by panel, Sounds like the Spanish inquisition. If I was successful at this interview that would leave only the uniform fitting and the routine medical, I attended the interview and did quite well. I was notified that I could now attend the uniform fitting and or the same day I could go for the medical.

The day of my uniform fitting it was very hot and I was sweating and tired. I tried on a number of crisp, white dresses in front of a long full length mirror. The face that stared back was very serious and with the uniform came an air of authority. I had lost some weight though still very overweight and I thought I looked quite reasonable.

It was at this minute that I realized just how close I was to nurse training and I was a little scared. I felt a surge of pride and I really wanted to be a nurse and for the first time I felt it with conviction, Lack of faith had prevented me from actually believing that the Lord could be right and that I could do it. I reluctantly took off the uniform and went for my medical, I was never ill and my medical history was very boring because I didn't have any. I had a routine blood test and was then allowed home.

I had just to wait for confirmation of acceptance to nurse training and the official starting day. was somewhat perturbed to receive a letter stating that the routine blood sample I had given had been lost and would I therefore attend the clinic and provide another one. A week later another letter arrived again, stating that the blood sample was unsatisfactory and would I please furnish another one. I thought that this letter must be a mistake but when I rung up I was told to come and give another sample, A week later ~ you guessed it; another letter arrived. the blood sample I gave had coagulated, please could I give another. I was beginning to think that the clinics were doing something sinister with my blood. Another letter arrived, guess what, the blood sample had been dropped and another letter the blood sample was insufficient quantity, whatever was going on if they wanted a blood transfusion there must be easier ways than this,

I felt very close to God at this point and I couldn't understand why. Things were going reasonably well in my life and as far as I knew I wasn't at some major crisis point so this really puzzled me. I expected a letter to arrive saying I hadn't been accepted for nursing and perhaps God was comforting me ready for any disappointment that I might feel.

I was eventually summoned to the hospital and told that I had a blood infection and that I should contact my local doctor who would explain further. I did this but he did not enlighten me any further. I returned to the hospital to discuss what was happening with regards my application for nurse training. I went to the clinic and the doctor there told me that I had Leukemia....... I do not remember much of the rest of the visit I just remember that it was often fatal. People spoke about it in a hushed whisper and it was cancer, I don't remember how I got home it was just as well that John was with me. The word echoed round my mind like a death knoll – Leukemia.......

John tried to console me but I felt like some sort of reject, I mopped around for some time waiting to turn into some pathetic creature of pity. The prognosis and the general consensus of opinion was that I would live for about three years. I would so miss John and the children, that's all I could think about. I would have to have chemotherapy and I would be sterile. I would be very ill and would have no quality of life as even the simple things would exhaust me. The anguish of the things I hadn't done, the time wasted, the opportunities I missed to be with the children. How would John manage without me and even now I have a lump in my throat when I think of the sadness I felt about it all.

I did not lose sight of God though and I prayed for guidance. Already it became clear how much the Lord loved me. He had joined me to John who helped me through all my earlier emotional difficulties. How getting pregnant so young and finding God when I was desolate. He had begun to build the foundations that would help me in this life taking crisis. I was puzzled because whenever I prayed the Lord was still showing me nursing. I had recovered from my bout of self-pity and when I hadn't turned into some kind of freak I contacted the hospital about still doing my nursing. The hospital was not too pleased about this but I wore them down and when they ran out of excuses they gave in, God putting His Plan into action, who can stand against Him.

They assumed that I would be too ill to cope with my training and would certainly be too ill to work and did not expect me to live for long. In a last ditch effort they sent me to a specialist Haematology Consultant in Manchester thinking that he would agree that I was not fit to do my nursing; instead he agreed with me and said that if I really wanted to nurse then I should go ahead and do it. The hospital admitted defeat and I was given my day to start training.

Nearly a year had passed since I first applied to nurse but I was very determined, after all God Himself had said to do it. Just as I was accepted John was made a redundant and this was a big blow to us. Financially we were very much worse off and John could not find another job anywhere. I thought this was a little unfair of God to deal us such a blow but as time went on it became more obvious why this had happened. It was a blessing in disguise as my training got harder and I had to cope with my illness, John took over the household duties and looking after the children allowing me to rest as much as possible. I often teased him about what a good wife he made.

So to recap ~ God is such a good planner. I found him because I was pregnant, I had both my children very young and by the time I was twenty-five I was sterile and could have no more children. As a married woman the chances of a rare form of Leukemia being found through a blood test are very remote as married woman don't usually have routine blood tests and my nursing proved to be a life saver as my leukemia was found on a routine medical examination. I am overwhelmed just how much the Lord has planned my life down to the smallest detail and all we have to do is just listen to him when he speaks to us and follow his advice. Blessed is God the Great Planner.

CHAPTER FIVE

The Ups and Downs of a Nurse

I began my nursing and was determined that I would do well. My first week was spent in school learning about the body and the various functions and systems that were involved. I was amazed just how intricate the body is and how like a jigsaw all the functions complement each other perfectly; it's all so precisely planned and so accurately that you cannot be but amazed by it. It was a bit like being at school again and the stress of the end of the week examinations were interspersed by the odd practical joke. The skeleton was dressed up in someone s best suit and to be honest it looked quite handsome. Another trick was to swop the urine samples for testing with other substances such as alcohol and cold tea the results were quite amusing as well, to practice moving patients we either practiced with each other and with this so called life - like dummy. The dummy, called dora, had this annoying habit of; whilst in the middle of a serious demonstration, chucking its leg or arm onto the floor and reducing us to hysterical giggles. We would often swop its bits and pieces around much to the annoyance of the tutor. The dummy could be adapted to male or female and one of its additions could turn it into a male. This too had the nasty habit of dropping off at the most awkward moments for instance when we were giving a demonstration to a group of visiting dignitaries and the offending appendage dropped off at the feet of the visiting mayoress; much to our very obvious amusement.

I often think back when we were doing a blood pressure and recall how we worried in those earlier days as we practiced on each other. The struggles we had to find each other's blood pressures; is it too low?, is it too high? or even oh I can't find; it you must be dead. The taking of temperatures was taken very seriously and the finding of the pulse had to be so accurate. Now we find them without thinking about it and it is very rare that we cannot read a blood pressure.

The exams were done at the end of the study weeks and for our first it was quite an ordeal. Always in the back of your mind was that if you failed twice on a row you would be a thrown out in disgrace. The first exam I only just scrapped in on the minimum score, the second week I prayed very hard the night before the exam and did much better much to my utter relief.

Friendships were formed and a person's character underwent a considerable change. Nursing took up a great deal of time both during the day and even in your social life. Many didn't realize just how much time and effort is expended in nursing. You finish your shift too weary to go out or you need to study. You finish the day where your favourite patient has died and you can't shake off that feeling of despondency. Your boyfriend wants to go out on Saturday but you're working. The amount of boyfriends that fell by the wayside was worrying. Gossip was about the boyfriend's lost and found, the children's progress at school and how is Mrs. so and so in the third bed. If you listen to a nurse's conversation at meal times you would never eat another thing. I listened to it all and I watched as each person developed a style that would help them cope with all the variations of nursing. We as the new bunch, were very conspicuous with our new uniforms, with the regulation shoes on and the right badge and our hair pinned up. How we worried about the way we looked, about our exam results, about our first day on the wards and how it would; we never would be nurses we wailed as we put Dora, the dolly, on the bedpan the wrong way!!!

How our hands shook when we gave our First injection into an.... orange, we spent fifteen minutes drawing up the fluid correctly. Not long after we were so nervous in our first attempts we would take two seconds and deftly slip it into someones skin whilst discussing the film seen the night before.

I was doing better than I expected, I felt quite well and nobody knew about my illness except my tutor, It had been decided not to tell the ward sisters as I was not want to be treated any differently than the rest of the class. I went on for a little while before my disease began to develop and was out of control, I had to see the consultant at the hospital at Manchester every two weeks and this was proving difficult as I could not have any time off without the risk of being told to leave nursing as had clearly been pointed out to me. The ward sister eventually heard about my problem through the hospital grapevine and would give one of my days off on the day of a hospital appointment, This sorted out the problem of my hospital appointments but it often meant that one of my days off could be at the beginning of the week and the other at the end of the week. It was quite a strain to keep this up. I never got the benefit of two days off together so I could rest properly, it meant that I was working at a hospital and also visiting one on my days of. We rarely got weekend off as students and I found this very draining and I found it difficult to study.

I remember my first ward very well, the very first day on the ward I came on duty at twelve o'clock and was to finish at nine pm that night. I was very nervous and unsure of myself and as I had no idea what to expect. The Sister for the ward was dashing about and when she saw me she looked me up and down and told me I looked very sensible and said I'd do. I was escorted off with another nurse where I was taken behind some screens and there lay my first sight ever of A Dead Body. I'd never seen a dead person before and here was I expected to help clean and lay out the body. I'm glad that the person was a stranger to me I think this made it a little easier for me. It's much harder when it's a patient that you have nursed and come to know well.

Also on this ward I met my first patients with Leukemia. Most people who suffer with the type of Leukemia that I had are in their late forties, it was considered quite rare to have this form of the disease as young as I was, Initially I was prevented from nursing them as it was thought that it would be too de- stressing to me as they were all terminal cases and it was just a matter of how long which was individual to each person, eventually I was allowed to nurse them and there was two men in particular who helped me cope with my own disease because of the way that they coped with their own. They knew they were dying slowly but they had a quiet acceptance of this and did as much as they possibly could within their limitations. Tiredness was a major factor in their day to day living and also recurring infections which took a toll on their health. I had long discussions with both patients which I believed helped us all. They had someone who really understood what they were feeling and I was less fearful of how my disease was progressing because I knew what to expect. I learnt from my own experience about caring for people who are ill and my illness gave me a rare insight into people's problems. I tried to apply the things that I had learnt to the patients and also to apply the compassion and understanding I felt in all my nursing. I was to attend a London hospital before commencing drug therapy. It had been decided that whilst my leukemia, was in an earlier stage some of the blood would be removed and stored in liquid nitrogen and re-introduced into my blood when my disease had reached a later stage, this would give me some extra time and the disease would revert back to the earlier stage. I attended the London hospital and despite the rail strikes I managed it without time off work much to my relief.

I began the drug therapy and for a while it made me feel very ill; eventually the side effects reduced and I had to be very careful about getting in Infections and had to be very careful how I nursed certain types of diseases, I was so careful that I rarely got diarrhoea or vomiting which plagues all nurses at some time. I got stuck into my nursing and studying and time soon passed.

I moved onto a children's ward and this caused some concern, I was susceptible to some children's ailments particularly chicken pox or viral infections. It was very rewarding at times but there were great moments of sadness. To nurse a child who is terminally ill is very difficult; you have to keep part of yourself locked up a little. I was nursing a young girl with lymphatic leukemia, a type which is very common in children, she was very ill; she was a beautiful child but was so pale and so tired. She lay on her bed forlornly trying to smile. Her favourite thing was a battered little tin, which she kept a couple of shiny buttons and some bits and pieces. Her special treat was to get out a little battered gollywog that Robertson's jam used to give with their jam. I would tell her stories about it, it was faded and a bit scratched but she really use to like it. She kept it hidden under her marbles and a little dolly made out of a cracker, I heard that the gollywogs were no longer being made due to some fuss about them being considered racist.

I decided to write to Robertson's to ask if they had a little badge left anywhere that I could have, I told them about my little friend and how ill she was and left it at that. I received a knock on the door a week later and there was a parcel which stood about four feet high and about twelve inch across. When I opened the parcel inside was the most beautiful cuddly gollywog I had ever seen. It was really big, as big as my little friend. Also in the box were some new golly badges of doctors and nurses and a giant poster and a really long wall -frieze with the new advertising campaign on it them. The cuddly golly was an exact copy of the little girls badge and you couldn't put your arms round it, it was so big. I had been on a weeks holiday so I took the gollywog in to the ward when I returned, I was so excited and I couldn't wait to see her face. Imagine my distress when I saw her bed empty and when I asked I was told she had died earlier in the week. It took me a long time to recover from that. I left the huge golly for the other children and I gave the ward some of the posters and badges. I kept two of the badges, a little nurse and a little doctor to remind me of my friend. Thank you to the workers of Robertson's Jams who were so kind to an unknown little girl.

I shall go onto happier moments before my tears stain the paper. Every week an old man use to visit the ward on Fridays. He would bring a bag of sweets for every child no matter what colour they were or what religion or even what age they were. He even, brought some for the big children (the nurses). He would give out his little bags of goodies and just stop long enough to see the children's faces light up. He did all this out of his pension and he was a real blessing to us all. It was such a delight to see such a simple act bring so much pleasure to everyone. I really want to mention him and show you how much kindness there still is in such a materialistic world that we live in.

I was on the children's ward for some thirteen weeks and the travelling became very difficult as the paediatric ward was situated at another hospital. I had to live in the nurse's home for some of the time and just go home on my days off. I was often ill in the night and had to lie there alone and just cope with I all. I really missed my family at this time. I had a room next to the fire bell and the psychiatric ward was nearby and the patients were always setting their mattresses on fire so it was difficult to rest properly.. This would then set the fire alarms off in the nurse's block and on these occasions we would see some sights. Out of the back door would run the boyfriends, fiancés and even husbands and the nurses would meet at the fire drill point dressed in the weirdest attire.

I was on a strict diet whilst I was ill as my cytotoxic drugs were making me gain weight. The next room to my room was taken up by the dietician who was looking after me. I twice got caught sneaking past with a friend, also staying in the nursing accommodation, returning from the chippy which was round the corner from the hospital and there was no denying it as the smell of fish and chips wafted up the corridor, and my friend and I dissolved into hysterical giggles.

My health began to deteriorate somewhat I was still managing to do my work but when I returned to my room I was so tired I would often go to bed straight away and this would be about five pm. Thank goodness that John was made redundant and was at home to do all the things I just didn't have the energy to do. This was a positive thing being out of work. I would never have been able to continue without his help, I was still attending the hospital at Manchester and whilst there I was offered the chance of a place on a bone marrow transplant unit at Hammersmith hospital, London. Again God had planned in advance. One of the doctors I was under and who worked at the hospital I worked in contacted the London hospital and they seemed interested in my case, I was told I was very lucky as usually there isn't any chance of being treated in a top hospital in London, a chance in a million was how it was put, So having followed. God's guidance I had my children, I had my disease diagnosed and now had a chance of a treatment. I was truly blessed. wasn't I.?

The next stage in my life consisted of lots of various blood tests which had to be completed before I could be considered a suitable recipient, never mind finding a compatible donor. I seemed to revolve round hospitals at that time and life was pretty grim at times, some people who knew me were often unkind at times and often it was pointed out to me that I was neglecting my children and they would have no family when I died and would have very little family time to remember when I had gone.

I was under considerable pressures to give up working; I could not obtain any help financially or otherwise with my disease simply because I would not give up working, I did not expect to die and I so wanted to nurse when I was better and if I gave up half' way through my training I would have lost the chance to nurse forever, Many basic state benefits were there to ease my discomfort were denied me because it was considered that because I continued nursing then I couldn't really be could that ill. The rigorous tests went on and I ignored the criticism, I knew that if I stayed at home like an invalid I would have eventually got worse a lot quicker than if I continued working. I knew that God wanted me to carry on and He provides all you need to complete what is in his plan. The tests were completed and I passed all of the psychological and physical tests and it was now it was time to see if a family could be found who would be a suitable bone marrow donor.

CHAPTER SIX

The Lord provides a donor

My life was truly guided by Gods hand but at times it was clearly evident and at other times is was rather obscure or so it seemed to me. I could see clearly the circumstances which had brought me to the place of being offered a transplant place and. I could clearly see the Lord's planning in it but before that became right I had many difficulties to overcome and sometimes I could not see God's plan for me. How arrogant that sounds that I a mere mortal should be in God's confidence. I knew by now that I could depend on God's faithfulness and that all He promised would be fulfilled I often couldn't see the end Plan or the end of one of the paths it's a matter of faith to keep checking and keep going in the right path. He never deserts us no matter what the circumstances are or even what we have done and this gives you the courage to face everything with the knowledge of the love of God.

The problems began with my parents really. Thinking about the premise of taking time to see what actions have happened in the past and what led to what I believe that the Lord gave my Mother her baby when she was in her forties in anticipation of my transplant. I told my Mother that I had leukemia, she didn't seem overly concerned even though her own sister had died off' Leukemia only a year or so before (unbeknown to me at the time), I explained that to save my life I would need a donor and would they consent to my sister being tested, My sister was a year older than my daughter and she was eleven by now, and I needed their permission, my Mother thought that I was exaggerating the situation, I had consultants ringing her and writing to her to try to explain how desperate the position was and that they really would advise her to agree to Alyson, my sister, being tested. Meanwhile my brother who was old enough to give his own consent, had been tested and found to be incompatible and would not be suitable at all, The donor gives a blood test and then four main elements are measured, Each child gets a certain number of these elements from both sets of' parents and if less than four match then the chance of a successful transplant are **greatly** reduced, It took some time for my parents to grasp that my brothers marrow would not be suitable, It was some time before my parents agreed to have the tests done but eventually they did agree, I do not think on reflection that it was my parents aversion to anything medical that kept them from making the decision sooner. As our relationship was strained I did harbour thoughts of maliciousness which God eventually dealt with. I was told by a reliable source that my Mother sat in the waiting room looking like a. Victorian lady complete with pallor and a bottle smelling salts, I wish I could have seen it all.

Sometime later the tests were complete and guess what yes my brother was confirmed as incompatible and my sister proved to be an excellent match. Next began the long job persuading my Mother to allow Alyson to be my donor. I didn't see my sister very often and I sometimes wish that I could have returned home to help Mother to look after her and I would have got to know them both a little better, I did try it for a few weeks but I couldn't adjust to the lack of freedom or fitting back into another household, I was selfish at the time and if I had tried a little harder I might have eventually made a go of it. The cost of that attitude was that I had could have had a better relationship and I missed caring for my sister and I could have been closer to my Mother perhaps.

Back to the matter in hand, my Mother just did not want Alyson to be my donor, She seemed very hard to me at this time, even allowing for her anxiety out subjecting her daughter to some minor operation she was unreasonable about the whole matter, I got consultants from Manchester Royal and Hammersmith Hospital, London and the top leading specialist in the world to explain to her just what would be involved for Alyson. She would be placed under anesthetic and her marrow would be removed by syringes from sites in her hips and breast bone, She would be awake again in a couple of hours and she would feel some discomfort and aching in those places, She would be allowed home the next day, but still my Mother refused and the fact that I was terminally ill seemed to hold no sway with her. I waited and prayed for her to change her mind.

I had plodded on at work because I could do nothing except wait for my Mother to change her mind. It was now a month away from my final exam when I would become a fully qualified nurse, this last exam was crucial and I was very nervous about it, I had nearly completed my two years training and I would take this last exam and then wait two months for the result and then I had one last ward to do and. I would be a nurse. This exam was in June but in May my Mother had a change of heart and consented to Alyson being my donor. I heard that I would have to have the transplant straight away or I would not be fit enough to have the transplant and. I would lose the chance; I was terribly disappointed not to be taking my exam with the rest of my class and with what was involved in the transplant I didn't know if I would be able to remember what I had already learnt. We had a week in the nursing school just before I was due to go in hospital, it was our last one. I was very embarrassed when they presented me with a beautiful nightie and dressing gown and a little bag full of toiletries, it was totally unexpected, I finished work three weeks before my transplant to avoid any risk of infections from the hospital. I borrowed a video from the nursing school library on a couple of people who had transplants and it was pretty bleak viewing but John and I wanted to be Prepared, one of the patients actually died I 'found out later which didn't help our anxiety. John and I began to realize just what would be involved and we soon realized that we would require some help. We also began to realize that there was less than a 30% survival rate which was frightening.

We still hadn't any close friends and would be unable to rely on my side of the family and John's mum had enough to do to cope with her husband who was ill with heart trouble. We approached the local social services about being assigned a social worker as we anticipated that the children would have to be placed with a foster family while John was with me in the hospital, we were assured that all would be taken care of and that we should not worry about it. We provided easy to understand leaflets from the Cancer Research organization so that the social worker would be familiar with just what problems would probably occur and help could then be organized. We also contacted the social security as we would not be receiving any money from my work and would just have John's unemployment benefit. Again we did all we could to give them information so that everything would run smoothly and would eliminate a lot of worry for us as we would know that things would be dealt with and the children would be cared for.

It was at this late stage that John began to have doubts about it. One of the doctors at the hospital that I worked had told him that often patients went years and never needed any other treatment, Also this kind, reassuring doctor told him that the survival rate was very poor and that really I would have been better off just staying with the drug medication. He began to realize the risk involved and he agonized over life without me and even how would the children cope. He began to show signs of strain and the arguments that we had the week I was due to go were horrible. My son became unruly and was plagued with children's ailments and my daughter became very withdrawn. He had explained to the children that I was having this transplant and how ill I would be and also that their Dad may have to come down and help to look after me and that the children would be staying with a nice family for a couple of weeks or so. They took this very well and I was very proud of them as I watched them struggling with reluctance to go to people they didn't know and wanting the best for me, my son was very anxious and began to have bad dreams and sleep walking, he remembered that when I had to go to Hammersmith to have my blood removed, he had acute appendicitis. The local GP misdiagnosed the condition and he had to be rushed into hospital as the appendix had perforated. He was very poorly but I had to go the next day to Hammersmith and it couldn't be delayed. I was getting ill and soon the window to perform the bone marrow transplant would be passed. He always felt that I was deserting him at that time and here I was going away again and might not come home again and he needed me. It was awful for him and conscience rending for me.

The social services had done nothing about organizing somewhere for the children to stay, even up to the last few days they told us that we should bring the children down on the day before we were going to Hammersmith. On the day the social worker just stared at us as we turned up at the social services office with the children and suitcases. I ended up going accompanied by my brother while John stayed at home to wait or the social worker to arrange something for the children it was a very unhappy state of affairs. I remember well the day I left, it was about five thirty in the morning, very cold and damp. The children stood at the door crying and John stood at the door looking sullen and trying not to look concerned, they waved as I got into the ambulance and I wondered if I would ever return home again. I was so frightened at that moment', so afraid and alone, and thinking whether God would let me die? And what he had in store for me?

CHAPTER SEVEN

I Arrive

I arrived at Hammersmith hospital on a cold and chilly day which suited my mood exactly. This opening title sounds like a romantic novel doesn't it but that's as far as the fiction goes.

I was shown into the unit where I would spend six to eight weeks, most of it in solitary confinement. There was a main entrance and this was as far as the public was allowed. There was a little room where you discarded your outer garments and you sprayed your shoes. you were then given a plastic apron and a hat to put on, any bags or things brought in were sprayed with an antiseptic spray and when you looked like an alien you were allowed into the next part, You proceeded through a set of mechanical doors and into a long corridor that had small rooms that were leading off. Each room had a large window so that you could be observed without entering the room and some of the rooms had toilets and some did not, These rooms would be your 'cells' and inside there was. a small fridge and a colour television which helped you from going mad after being enclosed for some time. As I walked past these observation windows and thin haggard faces with saucer eyes peered back at me and it reminded me strongly of those the concentration camp images.

Each patient spent up to eight weeks in these little rooms, very few had an outside view. Each patient was advised to have a relative with them for most of the time and this relative was often the only contact with the outside world apart from the nurse who cared for you that day. Visitors were severely restricted to reduce the risk of infection and the nurses visits were kept to a minimum.

Also on the corridor was the nursing post where a nurse sat waiting to tend to your needs. There was also a laundry room which puzzled me for it was well equipped with automatic washers and driers, It soon became clear why this was needed but I'll tell you about that later. There was also a microwave which I thought was very luxurious until I was told rather sharply that anorexia and mouth ulcers were a problem and patients could arrange for something that would tempt them to eat to be cooked in it. There were strict rules with regards meals on the ward and food was subject to sterilization to prevent bacteria causing infections.

Also there was a dayroom which contained a large television and video and had a window that looked out onto the world. You only got to sit in this room in your first few days and your last week so it really was a treat. You could watch the whole world pass by that window. Many nationalities and some rather eccentric people live in London and. I found it fascinating. There were also visitors for the establishment next door which I was informed overlooked the nurses quarters and the name of this salubrious establishment was.... Wormwood Scrubs prison. If you refused your medication you were threatened with being sent there. I was told to make the most of this freedom as it would soon be coming to an end.

The previous occupant hadn't actually left my room so I was free to do as I pleased as long as I was available for the tests lined up for me, talk about the bed still being warm.

I had been to Hammersmith before but instead of staying in the hospital I had stayed in a lodging house near the hospital, These lodgings were quite near to Shepherds Bush Green and I saw the theatre where Top of the Pops is broadcast from and there would be lots of teenagers waiting at the back door to see the groups arrive. It is also were the Terry Wogan show is filmed from but there weren't hoards of teenagers waiting for Terry, I had hoped I might be able to sneak out and look round at Shepherd Bush market but it wasn't possible. I was taken to various departments to have my tests done and then told that I had finished for the day. I went to the day room and decided to watch a video, there was one in the machine already.

I just switched on the television and waited. The video of which there was only one, it being a new concept was E.T. not a. good choice really. The video recorder VHS was a very novel thing so I was looking forward to trying it. Each time the little critter said ET phone home, made me cry, my brother had left to go home hours ago and I was distressed. I really missed the children and John and this was only the first day and in fact even today I can't watch E.T. without that feeling of sadness returning and making me cry.

Eventually my room was ready, having been thoroughly cleaned out and sterilized, I thought it was rather novel to have my own television and fridge but the novelty soon wore off.

It was interesting to see how the nursing standards and routine differed from that of my hospital. The first difference I noticed was that you got cup of tea and a cake at 4pm which was really pleasant; we just took a big teapot round on a trolley and if we remembered you got a biscuit. Here there were individual trays and it was really nice. Another big difference was at meal times, we get a large heated trolley contained all the meals and we sit the patients at the table and we have to deal with all the aspects of sorting out the meals: in Hammersmith the meals are brought up on individual trays in special trolleys that allowed the trays to be stacked and domestic staff gave out the meals and collected in all the plates, trays and things, where at my hospital the nurses had all this to do themselves, very enlightening.

I really enjoyed it first thing in the morning because the hospital employs a large number of Jamaican ladies and they use to come in and begin the cleaning or whatever and they sang such happy songs, The lilting voices singing gospel songs really cheered me up, I soon discovered that there was a portable phone and I would spend ages talking to the children, They seemed to be coping but it was very hard to have to put the phone down because I just wanted to talk to them all the time.

I was allowed some lee way during that first week and spent the time exploring. I watched all the people coming and going as you will realize this is a hobby of mine, watching and listening to people. There were some trees in the grounds and it was amazing just how many birds there were and a little wildlife that lived in such a busy area and with so much traffic all about. I use to like going, sitting near the huge kitchens, the smells were delicious.

Next to the kitchens there was a tiny chapel, very simply furnished but it had such an air of peace and hope even amongst all that pain and bustle of the hospital, I spent many hours praying or sitting asking the Lord's help in this time of illness. Even then I don't think that I still fully appreciated what the Lord was doing for me but I trusted him. I still pop in on occasions when I go down for my outpatients appointments and capture that peace again and to give thanks for his help. The week of freedom passed far too quickly and before I knew it I was to begin the transplant in earnest. I little realized just what I was in for.

CHAPTER EIGHT

Bald is Beautiful

The treatment started now and there were no more jaunts about the hospital and I began my isolation, I began on the drugs that would, along with the radiation, destroy my bone marrow and all the cells in my body. The side effects I was warned about were extremely unpleasant and mainly consisted of vomiting and diarrhoea which would last for days on end. I was quite cheerful at first when the symptoms were mild but felt very bad when the effects got worse. I was rather intrigued with the unusual nursing procedures which I would never see in my own hospital and would watch avidly while they did their tests on me.

Each morning I would be woken at five thirty which I did not take kindly to though I am good at getting up early, medication would be given and then I could dose till eight then it was breakfast time, The meals on the whole were not as good as at home or the hospital where I worked but I think this is because of the size of Hammersmith and the varied diets required for the multiracial patients, Then it was time for the ritual bath and we were allowed out of our rooms. The baths were a little odd till you got use to them. They were like large china sinks with very high sides and there was a little step inside that you could sit down on. I remember being so tired later in my treatment that I couldn't step out of the bath because of the high sides and sat in the water for half an hour trying to summon up enough energy so I could get out.

On the way to the bath I would pass the windows were showed the faces of the other patients staring out, after a few days the patients would wave and try to smile. This was our only contact with each other and any information had to be acquired through a nurse. On the first night of my isolation I couldn't sleep and. I was watching the goings on in the cubicle opposite, Normally you couldn't see into the other cubicles but there were lights on and the man had taken a turn for the worse and he later died of chest complications which didn't help my moral any, it was sad to think of his death but the hope of survival for him was very poor, It really brought home to me just how risky this transplant business was.

Most of the patients were slim when they came in and went out thinner and bald not me though, I waddled in like a duck and waddled out bald and just a little thinner which was a bit disappointing, I asserted my independence right from the beginning, starting with the trip down to the radiation clinic. Each time they sent this trolley down to wheel me there I refused to go on it. The first few times I walked and then it began to be a matter of principle; I knew I was well if I could walk there and back. In fact, I managed it until right at the end when I just had to give in, this, may seem like a silly goal but it really helped me. I was very proud of this accomplishment.

Another week passed and this one really dragged on, the treatment was beginning to make me very ill and I wasn't the easiest patient as I do not like being ill. My sister was due down this week to give her marrow and also John, which I was really looking forward too. Eventually my mother and father came down with Alyson and John brought the children and was accompanied by my brother, all on the same train but my parents and Alyson insisted on taking a different train, crazy isn't it.

Was very worried about what John's reaction would be as I had been assuring him how I was all right over the telephone when in reality I was and looked absolutely ghastly, I didn't think that the consultant would let me see the children as there was always the risk of picking up some germs or infection. I was allowed to see them very briefly and then they had to be content with waving to me through the window and smiling. John was absolutely furious when he saw the state I was in and he felt I had lied to him and this made him very angry. I did it with the intention of helping him not to worry because there can be nothing worse than being told the truth and being three hundred miles away and not be able to do anything anyway, He was even more annoyed to think the doctors and consultant had never rung him once to let him know my condition and he had only my word for how I was progressing.

Alyson had her operation to remove the bone marrow and it all went well. The next day my parents popped in for a few minutes before they went to pick up Alyson as they were going on holiday for a few days. She was none the worse for her experience but I think she was very brave about it as she was only eleven, I had hoped my parents would take Carole for a few days when they got back but they said no, it was very difficult to understand really.

John arranged to take the children home end then somehow he would try to get back to me, The consultant had advised that a member of the family should now try to be present as the irradiation and the drugs can make the patients very depressed. John went to see the social worker assigned to us and told him that I was very ill and he was needed but the man never did anything about it. In desperation John took the children to his Mothers despite the fact that her husband was ill with heart trouble and she was troubled with arthritis. She had little option but to take the children which she did for though she is very hard woman I always say bless her for this to anyone who talks to me about her.

John returned to me and I was glad that he did. I was really beginning to feel so weary that I just lay in bed with not even enough energy to pour myself a glass of water. Sometimes I was given steroid drugs that really improved my condition; they were given and half an hour later I could get out of bed and walk around, I felt very cheerful and optimist when I could move about. I remember one young nurse new to the unit coming and telling me to get out of bed or this would make things worse for myself as I could develop a blood clot, I did try; and. she didn't need to be so very patronizing about it I fully appreciated just what complications could occur, but I couldn't get of that bed despite being the most stubborn person I know and I always tried my best and trying very hard... I vowed never to say that to a patient especially one suffering from acute anaemia.

I was beginning to lose my hair in great clumps and I know this bothered some of the patients but I'm not a vain person and with my Lancashire humour I saw the funny side of it, One night after a clump of hair had fallen out suddenly and fallen in some jelly I was trying to eat I decided to shave the lot off... I borrowed Johns razor and at nearly midnight we sat on my bed laughing as the hair fell off. The vibration of the electric razor was very ticklish and I have every sympathy for men who have to shave every day. It was a very strange sensation. When I was bald we found a scar on the top of my head which I have I never known about. At this time there was a new Star Trek movie out and one the crew aboard the starship Enterprise was a bald women I had her head, but I wish I had her body too instead of my dumply one... The next bit of fun was the wig; this rather nice gentleman brought this catalogue of N.H.S wigs and said I could choose one of them. After consultation with John we decided to have one that was silver/ white and had two long platts. If I had to wear a wig, I wanted a fun one. That nice man came back and wouldn't let me have one, I ended up with a dead ginger cat that looked pretty awful, To make matters worse the nylon hair was sewn onto a base which consisted of very course netting and when my little bristles grew they scratched against this het and was very uncomfortable and I ended up wearing a little headscarf tied at the back of my head and looked much more elegant.

The strain on John was beginning to show he was constantly arguing with the doctors and he was angry all the time, The doctors and nurses ignored him after a while and this made him worse. He needed some reassurance and someone to talk to but there was nobody. Hammersmith hospital copes with many world renowned treatments and does lot of pioneering work but on their transplant unit they never even had a counselor or a social worker specifically for that unit. I could see the agony that John was going through yet I couldn't do anything to help him, It took all my willpower just to stay alive. John would spend hours just sitting beside me and holding my hand and that was such a comfort, I was so weary by now I didn't think that I could go on. I'm a born fighter and still I hung on but I was slowly being drained of my life's energy, John was close to despair.

I had the odds shortened a little more by having two near fatal reactions to the drugs I was on and one severe reaction was my sisters marrow, One of the incidents was due to the incompetence of a nurse who read the instructions incorrectly for a drug she was giving me and instead of receiving the drug over forty minutes I got the full dose in just four or five. I was flat out gasping for air and very, very frightened, I rang the emergency bell for attention and five minutes later a nurse sauntered in and realizing the critical situation I was in she ran out after telling me to take it easy and not panic, If I'd had my wits about me I would have hit her. I don't remember much else after that I was given an injection that would reverse the effects of the reaction and then I was carefully nursed. I woke up the next day to find John sitting beside me with an ashen face holding my hand. I felt reasonably better and even managed a smile. He was so upset; he had only popped out to get a drink and came back to find all the fuss. I waited for the nurse who found me to come in and when she did I gave her a piece of my mind. Her excuse for taking so long to answer the bell was that she thought I needed a bedpan. I never rung for a bed pan I had one in the room and when I had used it I would leave it covered until somebody came in and then ask them to empty it.

My appearance had changed somewhat, I came in **very** plump, good skin and my hair recently permed and now I had bright yellow and red eyes, no hair and the side of my mouth and nose eaten away by a viral infection very pretty eh. I began to look like an alien, John would try to be serious and I would smile this funny smile and he would have to smile at the odd way I looked.

That's not to say amongst all this pain and anguish that I didn't have my little moments of fun, I had a special tube called a catheter inserted through my neck which went into my heart end came out under my right bust, It was supposed to make the introduction of drugs easier and also the removal of amounts of blood and would have eliminated the need for syringes and needles being poked into my skin or trying to get a blood sample when my arteries have collapsed.

It took the drugs all right but it wouldn't let any blood out and I was having at least two large syringes full removed each day. The team of highly intelligent doctors tried, all the means at their disposal but it didn't work. In the end they resorted to such technical necessities as tweaking the tube, ouch, lying me down with my head on the floor and my feet on the bed, flushing the tube with liquid but nothing worked, that's typical of me that is.

I was walking to the bath one day and I was connected to a drip which was hung on a drip stand. which I had to tow round with me, I named the drip stand Hector because I was very attached to it and it was rather like taking a pet dog for a walk all the time. This particular morning, I had a bad night and was feeling a lot jaded. I was shuffling past the microwave on my way to the bath when a cookery book fell off the top of the microwave and dropped open at my feet. With some difficulty I bent down to pick up the book when I noticed what recipe it had fallen open at, there was a recipe with a scrumptious colour picture and the recipe was for ~ Baked Marrow. I started to giggle hysterically thinking about all that marrow being put to better use, I was carted off by two very serious nurses who decided I wasn't fit for my bath and should be put to bed instead, I tried to explain but they just put it down to my off beat sense of humour.

While I was having my transplant and stuck in my little 'cell it was my birthday and to add insult to injury I had some birthday cards sent to me but I received a present which. I really was pleased about, I am an ardent fan of M.A.S.H.(mobile army surgical hospital) and never miss an episode of it if I can help it. John had written to Alan Alda (Hawkeye) and he had sent me a signed photograph taken by his wife and a beautiful letter which I have included, for you to read. Oh was I proud on that day. I also received a huge bunch o' flowers from the girls at the nursing school which I couldn't have because of the barrier nursing I was receiving but I could see then through the windows as one of the nurses showed me. Most of the people I knew had sent me letters and cards and I had many people praying for me. It really blessed me to think that they would take the trouble to write and pray for me.

I had no visitors only John but one visitor was a nun and her quiet assurance really helped, she would tell me about some of the previous 'inmates' and how they had got on. She showed me a picture of a model and she was doing really well. The most amazing thing was her hair, this girls hair had regrown jet black and the condition of it was superb. I didn't like the idea of having black hair being fair complexion person but I hoped it would grow as beautiful as this models hair had regrown. This nun did not bat an eyelid when I projected vomited over the bed and turned away discreetly as diarrhea ran rampant everywhere. She continued to chat like nothing had happened while I cleaned up the mess. She passed on information about a Swedish doctor who had come especially to Hammersmith for the expertise and the lady from China, there were people from all over the world and that's a sobering thought.

I was confined to bed by now and was slowly going downhill. John was still with me and he was my only visitor (from the outside world so to speak). Later on though a lady did visit me whom I had met on one of my previous visits and who I had written to on occasion she was recovering from a heart attack at the time and was only able to walk to the toilet on the ward When I met her she was sewing green frogs for a summer fete and I got to talking to her I was very popular on that chest ward as many of the patients were bedridden or restricted to just walking to the toilet while I was only there because that this was the only bed available; I was soon put to good use, I would get a shopping list ready each morning from everyone and then I would go down to the main entrance hall where there was a thriving shop which sold everything imaginable. I was very surprised and pleased when I saw her and again saw the hand of God at work. I was very worried as John had nowhere to stay as the lodging houses would only take him for a week at a time and they were now booked up with people who had booked their rooms earlier. He was also fast running out of money and this was causing some considerable anxiety which he could do without My friend, whose name is Mabel, had only seen me for that short time when we were patients together but she said she had a spare room and she would be willing to have him she didn't know John at all and hardly knew me and yet she offered him the hospitality of her home for however long he wanted it. She even insisted on giving him all his meals and she wouldn't take any money at all.

Wasn't that a glorious gift from the Lord., again He had taken care of us, I've got to know her well since then and we stay with her overnight when I come down to Hammersmith for my outpatients appointments. I hope that one day she will read this and understand how much she has done for us and how much it meant to us when we had no other person to turn too. Thank you Mabel you are really a remarkable person and I love you and your husband May God Bless You mightily. Thank you God for your care ….

CHAPTER NINE

I Meet My Father

I had another reaction to a drug and this time the effect was very serious I had a substance in a drip which I had before without any effect but in seconds of getting into my blood stream this drug caused all my systems to go into hyper-drive, within seconds I was in anaphylactic shock and fighting for my life. My body erupted into large yellow wealds and my head began to whirl I couldn't breathe and I must have become unconscious because I remember very little about that part of the proceedings at all. I felt that I was a lump of inanimate jelly all the pain and panic had gone and I felt I was in limbo feeling nothing at all.

I felt really odd and things didn't seem real somehow, my energy seemed to be draining away and I was thinking only of myself dying, for that is what I believe I was doing, it is a very selfish emotion. I thought of all the things that I would miss, the children, my husband, how I'd never been out for a meal or even gone dancing I'm not really a socializing person so this was really odd. I could hear everything that was going on, I could see the staff working on me and I seem to be looking down on the scene, John stood grim faced in the corner, I looked down and there was my body on the bed, I felt somehow that I was being drawn to a bright light–.

The light was brilliant but not in a harsh way and there seemed to be little shimmering lights within it. It's very difficult to actually describe such an experience. The next thing was I felt a hand on my head; I don't remember feeling surprised at all. I was filled with such a feeling of Peace and tranquility, such intense feelings of warmth and love. I heard a voice saying 'daughter your time is not right yet. I have heard your prayer I felt like I had been embraced and everything was still and beautiful, I felt energy returning to me I could hear the voice again speaking "You have been blessed with peace and tranquility and people you touched can receive that same blessing, Go and do the work I have for you".

I saw John sitting by the bed and holding my hand, he was alone and looked so desolate that my heart went out to him.. I wanted to stay within, this love and this light but I could feel that the voice wanted me to return. The light changed and I opened my eyes and was again in bed and was aware of John squeezing my hand, I watched a moment till he noticed my eyes were opened and then he held me in his arms until he squeezed the breath out of me. We gave thanks to God for sparing me:

I began to improve immediately much to the doctors surprise. It was hard at times but I was filled with a new strength and this sustained me I changed within myself' and my fear of dying was gone. My outlook on life was certainly changed, I drew on that inner strength many times and it never failed me. I received the last rites soon after my experience but I knew within me that I would not be in a position to need them.

I recovered slowly and my marrow began to take root, the consultant explained that my marrow was like a little seed and it had to be protected and natured, the cell count in my body grew very slowly but the cells were all healthy. The irradiation damaged one of my eyes and my skin was red and smelt of burning.. The irradiation also damaged the delicate skin in my mouth and my tongue. My mouth seemed to be just rotting away and my tongue was swollen and very painful. I was unable to eat and vomiting was still a major problem My nose was covered round the nostrils by a large weeping sore and the corner of my mouth was covered by what looked like a huge cold sore. It's difficult to believe that these problems could have caused me so much pain and were so dangerous. Later I went a really deep yellow which contrasted with the burnt skin and produced glowing sort of orange you could have painted me as a sunset, and my appearance left a lot to be desired.

John found it very difficult to cope but as I improved he seemed to be more angry than anything. Soon he wanted to take me home though I knew that I was too ill to go. He felt SO useless and he believed that when I was home he would be able to care for me. I had been confined to my room for nearly two months and I could see that John was struggling within this environment so I persuaded the consultant that I was well enough to go home. It was a Bank Holiday so there was no ambulance to take me home. I would have been put on a train anyway. We lied and said that there would be transport waiting at the other end. The train journey wasn't too bad as we had a first class compartment to ourselves due to the risk of infection the hospital booked a carriage. I had to wear a mask and I must have looked very odd with my little bobble hat and my red eyes and bright yellow skin, nobody would have sat near me anyway,

When we got into Piccadilly station we had a short way to go to the taxi rank and because it was a Bank holiday we couldn't get a taxi. We had to walk to the coach station and get on a coach home. The coach was packed and I had to sit squashed up with my suitcase on my knee. The journey was awful, there was all the cigarette smoke coming over me and people coughing all over me to say nothing about the constant stopping and starting; every jolt felt like a needle going through my bones. I just wish we had some friends or somebody we could ask to help us. When we got off the coach there was a journey of about ten minutes and then up a steep hill to our house. It took three quarters of an hour, each step I took caused me awful pain, my feet were still sore from the irradiation and I felt like I was walking on broken glass. I couldn't breathe going up that hill and when I think back I don't know how I made it, it must have been divine Help.

When I eventually got home the children were overjoyed to see me, they hadn't been told I was coming in case we didn't fool the doctors well enough. I went straight to bed and rested that day.

I remember my son hugging me so close that the tube I had still implanted in my chest really hurt but it didn't matter.

The hospital arranged for me to come to them twice a week, to do this I would go down one day stay overnight and return home the next day. I would then rest two days and begin it all again.

I spent a month like this travelling to and fro and barely existing and my health began to deteriorate. I was admitted again and it was found I was in acute liver failure and was seriously ill (not that I wasn't earlier!). John went home to look after the children and he was very unhappy about the situation. He really believed that the hospital wouldn't allow me home again because I would die there on my own, I spent two weeks with little improvement, my liver refused to recover. After two weeks I wanted to go home. One of the chemicals involved with liver function had just hit one of the highest levels recorded. The hospital did let me go home but I don't doubt they thought I wasn't going to survive. Most transplant patients do not survive at this level. When I returned, home I really felt the Lord close to me during this time and I kept telling myself and John that the Lord, had work for us, I believed this with all my Spirit and still do…

Eventually against all the odds and against all that I had been informed my liver began to improve though it took four years before I had a reasonable liver function, it is still very high and not working correctly but God has me in his Hand….

I began to slowly improve though it was a long and tiring process. I don't remember much about this period except that I had to crawl about for some time before I could stand up for any length of time. I spent most of the time travelling down to London for my hospital appointments, I remember too how when I had finished all my tests and treatments I was sent down to the outpatients department to wait for an ambulance to take me to 'Euston station and be put on the train home. The journey to the station was only half an hour at most but if I took a taxi, there would be no ambulance waiting at the other end and I could not manage public transport, On a number of occasions I was kept waiting for an ambulance from two to four hours just to take me to the station. I would barely recover from this when I would be going again.

There were brighter moments, I spoilt my children that Christmas and they were so good about being quiet and putting up with me. They tried to get me to eat which was so painful because of my mouth. My son would do a little dance that he had learnt at school, it was a little caterpillar dance; it use to make me smile. In his homework news book at school he had written...: My Mum went up to heaven but God and Mrs. God had gone to Asda so she came home. I really enjoyed that time at home with the children.

Physically I was very weak but I was determined I would get better and return to a normal life again. John cared for me marvellously but then we always said he should have been a nurse. The only major problem was when we had to go to Hammersmith he got very uptight and was very difficult to live with. He could not cope with the strain of going down there. He would get angry and unreasonable so eventually my brother would go with me. God made me incredibly strong in my faith, and when we are on our journey God does not promise us an easy road, indeed we are on the wrong road if it is easy but He gives the necessary Grace to make it through. John and I are working through this with His Help...

During these visits to the hospital I was told, that it would take about two years before I would be anywhere near fit to return to work, I knew that I would have to do it sooner or I would lose my place at the nursing school and would not be able to take my exams, I was on steroids and. all sorts of experimental treatment, one of my problems continued to be my mouth which was still just an ulcerated mess. I lived off Complan for months and I must wait patiently for the mouth to heal. My hair had grown some little bristles about quarter of an inch and I would wear a little woolly hat or a little scarf. I went into Manchester shopping with John and this was my first real day out, the weather was very hot and. I nearly collapsed, in the Arndale Centre. I felt dread-fully ill and had to go home to bed, I was having some problems with my skin and was warned that the sun could be harmful and to keep covered up. As the weather changed to cooler I also found that I was intensely cold all the time and struggled to keep my body heat. However, the problems were slowly being overcome despite the protestations from the professionals and people. But it was not in God's Plan...

John was struggling with his faith, not that he lost sight of God, but with the attitude of the church throughout my illness. He was a catholic at this stage. He wouldn't go to church though he felt very close to God. He was quite angry at the way the church had ignored our situation, despite they being aware of my condition had not been to see him. He felt the church was hypocrites, God had called to Him, but the fellowship of the body was missing. They preached about helping others, but nobody came to see us, or came to the house. The children were both in the school that was connected to the church but nobody showed the face of the Lord.

There was a lady who lived opposite, she was a member of our church, she had a large family, she cared about people and was a true daughter of the Lord. She would cook food for us, indeed if she thought we needed a coat she would give us the one that she had on. I thank the Lord whenever she comes to mind she was a wonderful person.

John rejected the church. I went regularly for a while and was glad to, but it worried me considerably that John was so adamant about not going. As my strength got better and my mouth was feeling a little better I took stock of what had happened to me. It's good to look back on what you have been through and how God has helped and planned things to the best. It certainly made me give thanks and be amazed by the journey with God.

I wanted to do from now, Nine months had passed and I was fretting about being away from nursing too long in case I got complacent and decided the easier route and stay at home. My mind was made up by a telephone call from my Director of Nursing. He told me I would not be fit to nurse and if he'd had his way I wouldn't have been nursing in the first place and that I should just hand in my notice. I would not get any special treatment and he was not going to make things any easier for me. That was the wrong thing to do because my middle name is stubborn and he just made me want to prove that someone like me could nurse. The Lord had made it possible for me to Nurse, my Leukemia and treatment made possible because I heeded the word of God indeed told me to go nursing so who was this person to say I couldn't do it when He was the instigator of the journey.

I was very upset and disgusting at his treatment of me and that he should threaten me in such a way. I had been assured that my place would be saved and not to worry about it. I had a real battle on to actually get back nursing. The Director of nursing would not accept a doctor's certificate from a local doctor but made me go all the way to London for it and then refused to accept it and lost me three months sickness benefit. He had examined me by a retired paediatrician who had no idea about bone marrow transplants and he passed me unfit to work. They did a lot of things to make it very difficult to return to nursing but the Lord cared for me and we overcame the difficulties.

An added bonus was that I passed my English o'level with an A grade Not bad considering that I had only been out of hospital a couple of months and just literally walked in and took the exam with no preparation and this was my very first exam The Lord certainly blessed me and His planning has had such far reaching effects even to giving my life back to me. I am amazed as I read through my testimony just how much He has guided me and planned out my life.

CHAPTER TEN

Crossroads Again

I won the battle and was able to return to nursing after quite a battle in January 1984. I was to begin on a female surgical ward which I was unhappy about, this ward had a hard ward sister and was unfamiliar to me. At the last minute, by the power of prayer no doubt, this was changed to a male surgical ward where I had worked before and the staff were familiar with me.

I hadn't been working long when I developed herpes zoster (shingles) which was potentially dangerous to me. Again I was very fortunate as I was due two weeks holiday and managed to recover somewhat before I was to go back on the ward. The pain was excruciating and would come on without warning; I would suddenly dash off into the toilets and bite the towel while the pain went down my leg. It would leave me very shaken and feeling quite ill but at least the damage was only temporary. The hospital were amazed that I had come through it so lightly but we know why don't we.

I had to do a further year of training to make up for the time I had lost and then I would be able to take my exam, I was sent next to the theatre where there is an odd lot of folk working with a rather off beat sense of humor. I really enjoyed it but I missed the patient contact, I only had the chance to speak to them for a few minutes before they were asleep. The staff, as I have said, were a little odd, they would put lubricating jelly in your shoes. You had special footwear to wear when in theatre and you left your outdoor shoes in the locker room, Also you had to wear special dresses and often they would hide your clothes while you were assisting in the theatre. When you were assisting you had to stand close to the surgeons table and they would sneak up behind you and drop things down your dress and there wasn't anything you could do. Another trick was the lid of the blood fridge, the water would condensate or the top and it was ice told, they would wipe it along the back of your dress and it was freezing, It was very enlightening working there.

I must admit that having my transplant had really changed my life, I too developed a rather strange sense of humour and my outlook on life changed too. I was a very quiet person, very shy and a little timid I suppose. No more, that all changed, you only have one life and you should take the opportunities when you can. I found that I could write poetry reasonably well and on the wards where I worked a mysterious poem would appear just Signed the mouse. There was a cute little symbol of a mouse on the bottom and the staff was desperately trying to find out who was writing them. I kept the secret for nearly a year and it was only till I was found doodling my little mouse character that the truth came out,. It was really funny watching when the staff, read the poems not realizing who the author was, standing right next to them.

I believe The Lord has blessed me with a talent for writing which is perhaps not as evident in this piece of work but I have managed to help many people with the poetry and short articles. I believe the Lord wants me to work in this area thought this is not to be my main work but healing. Anyway back to the subject, after a year was up I sat my final exam in October, the night before my exam I was frantically praying that I would pass I needed all the help that comes from The Lord.

I took three O'levels at night school whilst I was ill and doing my nursing, people often said to me how brave I was doing all that but The Lord gets the credit, He blessed me in abundance and more than answered what I had asked.

Well then all I had to do was wait for the results. The exam results came in first and I passed, all excellent grades. The week before Christmas I had the best present ever, I passed my nursing exams. I had some trouble getting a permanent job at first but eventually I was given a Post on the acute geriatric ward.

Also as if the Lord wanted to really bless me, John got a job as well. He hadn't worked for five years after being made redundant from a local cotton mill. He had been made redundant just before I was diagnosed with Leukemia and because of this I was able to do my nursing and he looked after the children and the housework. His new job was just what he wanted, it wasn't in a cotton mill but in a nursery and he was the caretaker.

It was a little odd how he got the job as well. He went for his interview and later was told he hadn't got the job, suddenly he was offered the job our thanks to the Lord that night we must have deafened him.

My health on the whole was quite reasonable but from time to time my sister's antibodies would attack my body as they were alien body to my body. My legs ulcerated, huge great craters from top to bottom and the underlying tissue became swollen and sore, I had to wear thick bandages for many months. My mouth had slowly healed over the year and was nearly normal. It had left me with thickened mouth tissue and where I had sores on my nose and mouth there was now pale craters left over the sites, I was quite ill on a number of occassions but I think this was because I returned to work so early and didn't give myself enough time to build up my strength. My arms were covered with brown patches and the skin had puckered up like burnt skin. I had to go on steroids for a long time and my weight has increased considerably. At the moment the main problem has been one of my eyes. It was damaged with the irradiation and is unable to produce fluid or tears which causes considerable problems such as blurred eyes and ulceration inside. I've had many treatments for the eye without success and am praying for the Lord to heal me. My legs are much better now and most of the other problems have begun to clear up. I was all set to plod along on the geriatric ward where there was a change again to the plan.

CHAPTER ELEVEN

Happy Birthday?

The Lord appeared ready now to move me on and the next stage of my development began to emerge. The day was my birthday and I was working till nine o'clock at night. I was volunteered as usual to work on the chronic geriatric ward which was short staffed. Whilst over there an old lady constantly needed to be lifted onto the commode, this was very difficult because her limbs were very stiff and rigid. I hurt my back whilst lifting the patient but I managed to finish the shift but the next day I could hardly move. I had to go to the doctors the next morning because of the pain I was in. A fine end to my birthday I mused. I had some muscular problem from strain and I was advised to rest my back and not work for a few weeks.

At the same time John had been talking to a young woman who worked with him and had been very interested to hear about the Fellowship which she attended. We discussed the possibility of going to see what it was like and we prayed on the matter. We were puzzled why the Lord was showing us it was time to think about moving on. We really felt the Lord say that we should go. We rang up as soon as we heard the answer to our prayers and did not realize that it was ten thirty at night but the young woman didn't mind. We agreed to meet on Sunday outside the meeting place and she told us that she had been praying at that very time in a small prayer group about us coming. Exciting stuff isn't it. To recap, I had my birthday on Thursday, injured my back the same day and attended my first Fellowship meeting on the Sunday. The Lord was going to give me a birthday present that I would never forget.

I remember that first Fellowship meeting vividly, if anyone reading this has attended one you will remember what a shock it is especially if you are from a formal setting such as Catholics.. First everybody begins by greeting each other with kisses and hugs. I thought there was no way that I would allow anybody to touch me like this. I put up my stand offish barriers up and felt safe for the time being. I waited for the sweet singing of hymns and was puzzled by the appearance of a rock band. The band began to play what sounded to my ears something between rock and roll and soul singing. I took a big gulp and stood and watched transfixed. I put a fixed smile on my face and hoped nobody would notice. John struggled worse than I did; we thought we had entered a place of fanatics and lunatics. Everything went from bad to worse as people fidgeting in their seats suddenly rose up and lifted their arms like a flock of demented pigeons. I changed my smile to my 'I'm cool and laid back about this 'look. The songs were choruses that were sung over and over and then people begin to clap in rhythm and started swaying to the music. I thought they might be learning them but the same thing happened over again. Perhaps, I thought, they haven't sung it well enough so they have to keep doing it. I looked at John and in our secret way we communicated our disbelief to each other. John's eyes took on a shell shocked look and he looked in pain. Oh boy what had we done? The congregation bobbed up and down like corks and I began to feel a bit queasy watching them...It didn't improve either because suddenly a woman launched herself, there just isn't a better description, into the centre space and began whirling and dancing. All the people began to smile and look even happier and then began to clap. I began to think I was in some Russian folk festival and then another woman joined the first. John and I decided it was time to sit down. The meeting went on for some time then suddenly ended, everybody began to leave but first they came and looked at us in a sympathetic and puzzled way, shaking our hands then going. John and I eventually left and

walking home we looked at each other and all we said was "Well"....
then we just laughed and agreed that we had just sat in a meeting
full of crackpots.

We prayed the following week about whether that was the right
place for us and again the answer came back yes. We were a bit
dismayed about this and then we were told that would do some
stirring up there now that caused us some worry. We thought it very
funny that we would make an impression on people like that little
realizing that soon we would become like they were and it didn't
take long.

The second meeting was exactly like the first but this time people
stood up and spoke in gibberish now that really bothered us. We went
home to check in the bible and began to understand a little better
what was going on. Our worship of the Lord was greatly uplifted and
soon we too joined the flock of peculiar birds and raised our hands
to the Lord and we felt a rejoicing in our hearts.

After a few weeks I still had not returned to work and I began to
realize that the Lord wanted it this way. I could not possibly attend
the meetings as I did because I only got one Sunday off in three or
four. I often had to work nine days and at least two nights till nine
o'clock and therefore wouldn't have been able to attend any night
meetings.

As I learnt more about the Lord I began to understand better
just what He had taught me by the things that had happened to me.
I learnt more about what He wanted from me and not just what I
wanted from Him. I began to realize that my faith was very strong
and that having Him and nobody else to turn to that my trust in Him
was also very strong. I learnt that the Lord is faithful to his word
always and that I should let Him use me and not put limitations on
myself which in turn limited what the Lord could do with me.

John struggled a bit at first because of his Catholic upbringing.
He was as strongly told to be a Catholic in his teens as strongly as
the Lord was telling him now what he wanted but John thought that
it was denying everything that had happened to him whilst he had
been a Catholic. It took some time before he fully realized that the

Lord had work for him to do and that he needed to learn more and that he could learn what he needed in the Fellowship. He struggled

for instance, to let people close to him and he found it difficult on occasions to express himself. He struggled to let people touch him and even now is rather reserved in his worship. He has no trouble if he sees a problem in tackling it no matter what sacrifice this means to him personally but he struggles in a group of people fitting in. He spent a lot of time in prayer and carefully considering what he was to do but eventually accepted that it was not a denial of anything past but simply a learning process and that the Lord wanted this for him.

About five months passed and we were attending a basic study course which we called a Foundation Course. We were taught basic Christian values and teachings and also the aims of the Fellowship. The group was only small and consisted of John and I and another new couple. The Lord really moved in that small group The first time we met, the Lord spoke to John about one of the members having had contact with a Ouija board and tarot cards. The group was taken by a leader and he, with our prayer support, cast out the spirit that was the problem.. It is very frightening to some to see these things done but I must admit that John and I it seemed a natural thing to do. The person we prayed for is now very involved in healing and can pinpoint a problem without knowing anything about the person being prayed for. I myself have developed in this field but I know that I am to be used in the healing of emotional and spiritual hurts. John appears to be developing a discernment to be used in Spiritual Warfare for which he needs to be strong.

During this Foundation course we were asked if we would be interested in being baptized and we attended a baptism of some of the Fellowship at our local baths. Each person was totally immersed under the water and when they emerged they were given new life in Christ. The atmosphere was electric and there was such a feeling of joy and it was very emotional and exciting. Each person wore white and spoke a few words then they were 'dunked' beneath the water by two or our leaders. The Lord spoke directly and clearly to John in a voice that seemed so loud that John thought that everyone could hear it. The Lord said this.... "After all I have done for you, will you not do this small thing for me ".

This really shook John up for the Lord had spoken indirectly to him in the past but not this time. John had been adamant that he would not be baptized because he had been earlier in his life. However after God speaking to him he changed his mind as a person just doesn't argue with God and listens if he is wise.

CHAPTER TWELVE

Water, Water Everywhere

God really is perfection at planning, our baptism coincided with our lessons about baptism and the work of the Holy Spirit, this was the first time this had occurred. I really thank God for this because everything just fell into place and it was really beautiful for us. Those in our small group also decided to be baptized and so did John and I. We had two weeks to prepare ourselves and to repent of anything which would hinder us and release any areas which we had not released to God.

John asked God to release him from the fear and anger which gripped him each time I had to attend Hammersmith hospital and which made him so irrational and difficult. He felt bound by the fear of losing me which had gripped him when I was so ill. He confessed it aloud; within the group which was quite brave for him and we prayed for him. He felt the release of this as if a weight had been lifted from him and he is actually better now when I have to go to any hospital, praise the Lord, for the stress that was caused because of this fear was dreadful, praise the Lord. I asked again to feel that compassion and peace which I had felt on my 'death' and to be refilled with the Holy Spirit as on the day of my baptism.

I had been told by many people that often the Holy Spirit grew after their baptism rather than an immediate overwhelming power. I believed that I would receive what I asked for and I would accept nothing less. It was a trying three weeks at least for me as doubts flooded into my mind, doubts that had not entered my head for years. Had I truly released my life to God or was I fooling myself. What if I was unworthy, what if this was something that I felt and not really from God. There was never any doubt about what God had done for me because I was alive and He had been with me on my journey; but the enemy tried to persuade me that I hadn't done what God had asked me at all and that my love for God was superficial and a sham. It didn't work; I drew on God's love for me and my trust in him and knew He was faithful always and that what He had promised would be mine. I prayed for a long time and I was rewarded. The Lord said He would heal me - I was still having serious problems with my transplant. From time to time my sister's marrow would attack my body and organs believing them to be alien to it. I had trouble with diarrhoea and parts of my body were breaking down all together. I was on many drugs which dampened down the attacks and one of these was a new drug which came in a little bottle which lasted me two weeks and cost about four hundred pounds. I was told that I would take some of these drugs for the rest of my life and it was vital that I take them; some of the drugs were on an experimental programme and could not be stopped without specialist medical supervision.

I really believed that I would be healed as God had assured me of this. On the day of my baptism I did not take any medication and knew that I would never take them again. I was baptized and it was a beautiful day for me. I was filled anew with the Holy Spirit and again I was filled with such peace and compassion that I had enough love for the whole world. It took me months before I came anywhere near earth bound and was tolerable in public. I felt so good and felt such a wealth of humanity that I felt I would explode. I now earnestly sought the gifts of the Spirit and I prayed that the Lord would continue to teach me and prepare me for them. I feel like I am being prepared for some great work which excites me and frightens at the same time.

I began to have health problems that soon developed into serious complications and my body began to break down. I became very tired and in pain, the diarrhoea was uncontrollable and my eyes became worse. I went to see my consultant but there was only doom and gloom and it soon became apparent that I would have to go into hospital, The hospital considered putting me in isolation and begin biopsies to determine where the problem was. I was given a couple of days to get use to the idea of going into hospital and arrange things. I prayed to the Lord to ask for help and the Lord told me not to start taking my medication again because everything would be alright.

I was very worried about my condition and I really thought about taking my drugs but I didn't. Two days later my condition began to miraculously begin to improve for no reason. My improvement was very dramatic and I believe that the enemy was trying to get me to disobey God and destroy my trust in God. It didn't succeed and I have continued to improve and the only problems that remain is one of my eyes, damaged by the radiation still does not lubricate properly and this causes internal damage sometimes, and the skin on my legs is still in poor condition but at least it is not ulcerated now. The Lord, I believe, will heal my eye in His own time and as for my legs I have just realized that I haven't actually asked about my legs at all I have for the most part written and typed this testimony with very little vision but I know I cannot move on until it is done.

I have become more involved within the Fellowship and have initiated a healing group which is doing very well and in some cases we have had spectacular healings, I have a disabled baby which I Pray for regularly and whom I believe the Lord will heal but really He wants the whole family. One of the group members was healed of a very painful back which had bothered her for years. A couple of months ago she gave up all her invalidity benefit and began to look for work. She hasn't been successful but I believe the Lord wants her to work with children in a special situation and this will be achieved soon.

I have been developing more in the realm of inner healing and emotional problems and the Lord is bringing people to me in unusual situations in respect of this. I am praying about the possibility of entering counseling and waiting to hear whether this is in fact what God intends for me. I have now left my nursing and did apply to the University for social work but the day of the interview everything possible went wrong from me having raging flu to all the buses putting me off at the wrong campus, If the Lord had wanted me to go there I think that He would have given me another opportunity to do it but nothing had occurred to make me think this is right.

Again I wait at the crossroads and it has now been a year since I hurt my back and I have progressed in the Lord but I am not sure where to go now. I know that this testimony is part of the waiting and whether or not it is published is immaterial to me because I have learnt a lot from just typing it and being to look back just on what the Lord has done for me. I have delayed the completion of this by many months but it was only just recently that I realized just how important it was to get it finished. I picked it up some months ago and I spent a couple of days just none stop writing and typing. I felt really good about getting so much done and a couple of days later I received a cheque from the Inland Revenue for quite a tidy amount which I had no idea about and which was owed to me from two years ago. The cheque arrived a couple of weeks before Christmas and I thanked the Lord for this blessing. I did lapse again from typing this testimony out for quite a while but have now nearly finished the book.

I have had many doors opened to me from people needing my help and I believe that the Lord is using me as an Ambassador. People tend to switch off when you talk to them about religion but illness gets their interest without any barriers being put up. People are always interested in what is happening to other peoples.

I attended a ten week evangelical course on getting on with other churches and learning about how to bring people to God without frightening them. I learnt that I am very fortunate in having a husband who is as committed to God as I am for I saw a lot of problems for wives or husbands who spouse is not a Christian. I just didn't realize how difficult it could be if a person wanted to attend a bible meeting but couldn't have constant nights out because of lack of understanding by their partner. I thank the Lord for John who I must have taken for granted on occasions but God knew we would be ideal for each other.

I also learnt about not placing limitations on myself and therefore restricting what God could do with me. I learnt that to be an evangelist you don't have to know hundreds of bible quotes or all the books of the New Testament by heart but that you can do it very effectively just by being yourself. I learnt that my most important asset in this work is my own testimony. Previously I had tried to be modest when people asked me how I had managed or how brave I had been, I just don't like being in the limelight at all but now I say yes it is amazing but I couldn't have done it but for God being there with me. I am not in the limelight at all but God is and that weary phrase giving the glory back to God has now some meaning to me. I have been responsible for not giving God the glory but now all that has changed and I willing talk about my ordeals and I talk about all the things which seemed insignificant at the time and how vital they were to me within is plan. I clutch the Lord's hand very tightly now but He is changing my personality to something so completely different from my quiet old self that it is unbelievable.

I am becoming more aware of the battle against evil and spiritual warfare it is interesting to me at the moment. We have a spiritualist hall nearby and we believe that it will be finished soon and that we will claim the land back in the name of the Lord. John has stood outside the hall and handed out literature to help the people realize that what they are doing is not what God wants. It was very nerve wracking at times but it needed doing.

John is involved in work with children and hopes that he will be able to open a youth centre in the area to cater for anybody with any problems i.e. glue sniffing or drug abuse. The Lord has confirmed in many ways that this is what He wants John to do and it is my role at the moment to help him establish this.

I feel that my writing will be very important in my work but not perhaps the most important aspect of what God has for me to do. I wait patiently for the Lord to reveal the next stage of His plan for me and hope that I am ready to do it.

Our local Fellowship has become involved in renovating a derelict building to use as a restaurant and counselling centre and I hope to be involved in the work there in some way I felt a little useless during this renovation stage as I am not particularly gifted on the practical side of things. I did however write to Cliff Richard about our plans and he sent me the autographed photograph which was a real blessing and encouragement to people. I hope that in some way I have been able to help somebody by writing this and even if it is only one person it will have been worth all the struggle. I want everyone to know the joy of loving the Lord and that they too can experience this incredible peace that I have and this love for people which brings such order to my life. I hope that I have demonstrated that all types of people can come to know the Lord even as stubborn and reserved as my John. A friend of mine who believed in God and had even been a Sunday School teacher in her day didn't understand about Jesus being the Son of God; yes he was a great prophet but the Son of God.,... One night lying in bed she was filled with the Holy Spirit and since then her life has changed. She has a friend in Egypt and she hopes eventually that they will marry. The relationship has been very difficult at times despite continuing for over nine years. They are now much closer, my friend worked as an auxiliary at a local hospital which was very hard work and left little time for her to enjoy her home life. She began to attend a local church; she was hoping to continue her earlier work in the Sunday School but this did not work out. In one swoop God gave her an office job in the local town hall, she has become involved in local church activities as she has more free time and weekends off. She feels so much better for not working so hard physically. I am happy she has found Jesus and is more content and happier. I want it recorded that I love her and I thank the Lord that He loves her too....

I have changed from the timid, withdraw little mouse (the mouse is my nickname) to a quiet (some might disagree) listening and loving mouse .... But when the Lord wants something done The Mouse roars like a lion....

And on this note I will finish and just say that the Peace of the Lord be with you...

Oh and keep an eye on the sequel because God has continued on His plan for me....

PHOTO BY ARLENE ALDA

Signed photograph of Alan Alda I gave it to Loraine on her birthday

Alan Alda

April 4, 1983

Dear Loraine,

    I've heard that you're not well and that you're in a very tough fight and I just wanted to cheer you on.

    I hope you grab every minute you can to laugh or feel the warmth of the people who love you - or give them some of your own warmth. They're the kind of minutes we're here for. I hope you gobble them up.

    Be tough. People are rooting for you. And remember to keep laughing. I'll try to take care of the last part from here.

                Sincerely,

                Alan Alda

Loraine with our children John and Carole
When Loraine passed the Nursing Qualification

Loraine being baptized

GOD THE GREAT PLANNER

PART TWO

THE JOURNEY HOME - DAUGHTER

© John Gibson

INTRODUCTION

My name is John Gibson the husband of Loraine Gibson, the author of **"God the Great Planner"** Part One. I am having to write part two because Loraine went home to God on 29th November 2013 aged 58. It isn't easy for me to write the second part of Loraine's life because I am not a writer. For most of my life I was dyslexic and when I met Loraine my self-confidence was at its lowest. When I told Loraine I was a dyslexic I was amazed that she still wanted us to get married; confirmation that God brought us together. I do feel it's important that you know how Loraine continued her walk with God.

I can only echo Loraine's words that she gives in the front of this book *"I hope that my testimony encourages you to trust where God leads you and to believe that He has such power and ability to help you on your journey, **even if you cannot see where it leads**."* I hope that this book inspires you to believe in Jesus as your Saviour and if you give your life over to the Lord he will guide you through your life and help you to have it more abundantly.

John 10:10
10 The thief does not come except to steal, and to kill, and to destroy. I have come that they may have life, and that they may have it more abundantly.

NKJV

As part of this introduction I am including three articles Loraine wrote in the Nursing Times Magazine:

- ➢ Chronis Meyloid Leukemia (Published June 8, 1983)
- ➢ Bone Marrow Transplant – Process (Published January 21, 1987)
- ➢ Bone Marrow Transplant – Recovery (Published January 28, 1987)

Loraine wrote them from a student nurse's point of view and that of a patient's point of view. I've included them in the introduction so that you can get a better idea of who Loraine was and what made her who she was.

CHRONIC MYELOID LEUKAEMIA

Nursing Times Magazine June 8th,1983

Loraine Gibson, a pupil nurse, has been diagnosed as having this condition. She gives her thoughts and feelings from both a nurse's and patient's point of view

A PROVISIONAL diagnosis of myeloid leukaemia is made after examination of a blood sample reveals a large number of leucocytes. Upon this discovery, a bone marrow specimen is obtained from the sternum under local anaesthetic. If the patient has leukaemia, the cells will show chromosomal changes.

Outward signs of the disease are tiredness and weakness, unexplained bruises or excessive bleeding. Often the spleen can be felt, as it is usually swollen. The patient might be thought to be anaemic.

I was diagnosed in the early stages of the disease after a routine blood test. I am still managing to work although I do have to make concessions in my life so I can keep going.

After the diagnosis was made I regularly attended the staff clinic for blood tests. Only the staff health department and my director of nursing were aware of my problem. Initially I had been told that I would begin drug therapy when the number of leucocytes reached a particular number. Eventually the blood tests revealed that this number had been reached, and I was now to attend a small haematology clinic attached to a nearby teaching hospital. My first visit to the teaching hospital — after the initial diagnosis in the staff health department — was somewhat traumatic as I had thought my disease and its consequences would be explained to me. But I was told nothing. However, the doctor at the staff health department talked to me later and gave me some information about the disease, and advice as to how I could carry on nursing for the time being.

I was to receive the drug busulphan (Myleran). This reduces the number of leucoytes to normal so slowing down the progress of the disease, and at the same time the spleen goes back to its normal size. Unfortunately there are some drawbacks to using a drug such as this. One disadvantage is that the drug cannot differentiate between healthy and damaged marrow. Hence there are problems about using it long term. As I am only 26, the risks to me are considerable.

HOWEVER, there is now a new approach to treatment. This involves removing the leucocytes at a very early stage in the development of the disease and freezing them in liquid nitrogen. When it is becoming difficult to control the disease, the patient is given the stored cells and so the disease reverses into its chronic stage. However this measure is only a stopgap in that a little time is gained.

The consultant at the haematology clinic mentioned that one of the London teaching hospitals specialised in this technique and suggested I take the opportunity to go there.

I agreed, but with having to make the long journey from Lancashire to London I had to mention my problem to my ward sister. She was very sympathetic and helpful and in fact I felt better for being able to tell somebody at work. Furthermore, I was working in a geriatric ward at this time and the work was very demanding physically which meant I got very tired, and I felt I had to give some explanation for this.

I was to go to London three times for treatment, and I found the travelling tiring. Because of the train strikes at this time I was forced to stay in hospital for four days. During this enforced stay I became a little depressed, but being a patient made me appreciate a little how people in hospital feel. I think the worst problem was the total inactivity which leads to boredom which, in long-stay patients, can lead to a state of despair.

So it was not very long before the novelty of unlimited rest had worn off. I found myself, even after a few days, waiting anxiously for meal times, not because I was hungry, but because of the welcome break each meal provided in the routine of the day. Also, meal times provided contact with the nurses.

I think my enforced inactivity affected me more than it did most of the other patients, as I am used to being a participant in the bustle of a busy ward and not just an onlooker. However, I learnt many valuable lessons during my stay because the patients were unaware that I was a nurse and so talked frankly and openly to me. I learned that patients' grievances, even one as seemingly insignificant as not getting the bread and butter which was ordered, can be blown up out of all proportion. Even more important, I learned that a smile from a nurse, or a few moments spent chatting, are like golden moments in an otherwise routine day.

Sometime in the future I am to have a biopsy from a site near my hip and I must admit this worries me. I am also awaiting the results of bone marrow tests on my brother and sister and hope that the tests will show one of them is compatible with me. I have been told that there is a one in four chance of compatibility.

What I have described above happened in about six months and has left me very confused and bewildered. However, a word about the routine medical which most nurses tend to moan about because it always seems to come round at an inconvenient time. It was owing to stringent medical checks that my disease was discovered in its very early stages. I have had much help from the staff health department at my employing hospital. This department is as unappreciated as the regular medicals, but no less vital. The staff make my travel arrangements to London at short notice, have given me endless moral support and explain, where possible, some of the tests I have had to undergo. They have also arranged to do my weekly blood tests so I won't have to travel to the teaching hospital.

THE symptoms I have at the moment are really not as noticeable as they will be later on. I am extremely tired, but I am reluctant to tell the ward sisters about my disease as this might affect their attitudes towards me, or my ward reports.

I have been unable to enjoy a full social life as I need a great deal of rest when I get home. However, since I have left the geriatric ward I find work a bit easier.

I am reluctant to have time off work as this might affect the length of my training and when I can sit for my finals.

I had not anticipated the amount of travel I would have to take to hospitals and I have to try to take my days off when I have an appointment. This has called for some ingenuity on the part of my ward sisters but has been managed.

SOMETIMES I feel very despondent. I would love to be able to get on with my work but something always seems to crop up which makes it difficult to forget my problem. I hope I will get a respite from the tests some time so that I will be able to concentrate on my assessment in my next ward.

I am now adjusting to the thought of a possible marrow transplant even though this means a break in my training and an absence from my family and all the problems this will entail.

The curious thing about having such a serious illness is that as a nurse I have a thirst for knowledge about it while the patient in me tries to ignore what is happening.

Having myeloid leukaemia has certainly made me a more understanding person, for I realise better the hopes and fears and the feeling of bewilderment that patients in hospital experience when confronted with a situation much of which they do not understand.

BONE MARROW TRANSPLANT—
THE PROCESS

Nursing Times Magazine January 21ᵗʰ, 1987

IN 1983 I wrote of my experiences as a patient and nurse when diagnosed as having chronic myeloid leukaemia. The diagnosis was made after a routine medical to enter nursing. I finished the article at the point where the bulk of my training was complete and I was feeling rather pleased with my progress, both medically and academically. I had only a month to go before my final exams and I was being considered as a candidate for a bone marrow transplant at Hammersmith hospital.

A great deal has happened to me since then. I passed the strict criteria required for inclusion in the transplant programme, which were being under 40, in first remission and psychologically able to cope with the stress involved. I passed the strict medical required to rule out any underlying disease which could limit the success of the transplant. In fact, my medical was very boring and normal, all I had was a mouth ulcer. Well you can't win them all.

I attended out-patients and routine bloods, chest X-rays and thyroid tests were performed. All the results returned within normal limits, and my only claim to fame was my leukaemia. I had to have a narrow aspiration from my iliac crest. This procedure proved to be very painful and difficult. I am well padded in that region and after a number of unsuccessful attempts I was getting a little agitated.

Eventually I had the aspiration from the sternum as usual and, as usual, it was successful on the first attempt. I retired rather gratefully to my lodgings for the night.

I returned to out-patients the next day to complete the sequence of tests, lung function being most important because of the risk of pulmonary complications. The last test was the dreaded height and weight.

I was admitted to the transplant unit at dinner time and saw the last occupant of my room leaving, looking quite pleased. A video was available in the sitting-room (soon to be out of bounds to me) and the film showing was ET. I was alone and miles from home and the little mite saying 'phone home' reduced me to tears. I was shown my room with its fridge and colour television. The first visitor was the surgeon who explained I was to have a catheter inserted in my chest called a Hickman line. The catheter allowed the large amounts of blood to be removed without constantly pricking the skin and thus reducing the risk of infection. The catheter also allowed drugs to be given, rather than through a Venflon in my arm.

I had my first taste of rising at 5.30am and felt a twinge of pity for all the patients I had woken at that time myself. I was given a radio-opaque dye for a scan of my spleen which was to be done later in the day. I was shown where I would receive my irradiation, but the technicalities totally eluded me. I was to receive half-an-hour on each of three days. This sounded insipid enough, but I couldn't have been more wrong!

I had my limbs measured very carefully by a giant technician and I had to place my five foot on a chair so he could see me. The possibility of bone shrinkage was casually mentioned and I had visions of a four foot dumpling emerging. My spleen was next and, though it was a little higher than expected, it was discovered. I could see its outline on the monitor, and its position was marked on my skin. I was placed on a table with a huge machine beside it and could see a pit beneath the table which allowed the table and machine to be manipulated. The sight and thought of the pit made me very dizzy and disoriented. I had nothing to hold on to and I was very frightened. I didn't say anything as I thought a nurse should know better but I was very glad to get up when it had finished.

The spleen scanning had taken more time than expected so the dreaded catheter was left to the following day. I went for my first total body irradiation (TBI) and was worried in case the dizziness recurred. I lay on a trolley while lead blocks were placed to protect my eyes and cranium. All I could hear was a faint buzzing and little clicks and I wondered what all the fuss was about.

I spurned the wheelchair and walked defiantly back to my room. I then went to theatre and was met by the surgeon who spoke and looked like Sean Connery, which I found rather novel. An incision was made in my neck and the catheter passed into my right atrium and out through my right breast. I watched with the curiosity of a nurse and the anxiety of a patient. It remained in situ about 12 weeks and I nicknamed the strange little tube Humphrey. I became very attached to it.

I was very complacent at this point; I was not vomiting and I felt quite well. Later that day the vomiting began and I was given anti-emetics which helped. I started cyclophosphamide which aggravated the vomiting and I felt a little sorry for myself. I continued with the TBI and was determined to walk back on my own two legs; it became a matter of principle to do so.

But nothing quite goes according to plan with me, and the catheter would not allow blood to be withdrawn. The infusion fluids went in without problem but no blood would come out. Anticoagulants were introduced to no effect, and a number of other highly technical methods were tried, such as lying in a head down tilt and twisting and tugging the tube.

In between lethargy and vomiting, I had bouts of cheerfulness and determination. I had a bath each morning in a large square bath with a little step in it to sit on. It was the only time I ever left my room and it was a treat to peer at the occupants of the other rooms and wave to them. In this small corridor was a microwave oven, which I was informed, was to tempt patients into eating, as anorexia was a major problem. A good idea, so I shuffled myself and my drip stand over to inspect it. My dripstand lagged behind me like a faithful hound and knocked a scrumptious full colour cookbook onto the floor. To my amazement and mirth the book dropped open to reveal a superb illustration and recipe for...baked marrow! The nurses were puzzled by my loud, hysterical giggles. They put it down to my Lancashire humour. I developed hot and cold flushes and a red rash over my entire body.

I was having cyclosporin, a new drug being used as an immunosuppressant and which had improved the success rate and rejection problems immeasurably. I had intravenous fluids to combat the dehydration from the vomiting and anorexia. At midnight, while the cyclosporin continued, blood samples were taken and I often wondered in my dazed state whether the doctor was a vampire, as he kept such odd hours and took so much blood.

My sister arrived and under a general anaesthetic had small amounts of her marrow removed from different sites. I was now strictly barrier nursed as my blood counts fell. I received my first pack of marrow and, of course, a complication occurred. I went into severe anaphalactic shock which was so sudden I was caught unawares. My chest suddenly felt as if a great lead weight lay on it and I could not breathe. In seconds I was confused, panicking and frightened. I was given Piriton and hydrocortisone and slept the rest of the day. The reaction was because my sister was A-negative and I was AB, and we were not as compatible as thought.

I missed my family dreadfully and this was the first time my husband and I had been separated since we were married. I did wonder if I had made the right decision about the transplant, instead of seeing how my leukaemia developed. I was feeling low, depressed and ill.

My colour had changed to a dingy yellow from a scarlet red and my mouth began to break down at an alarming rate. The inside of my mouth became raw and was incredibly painful. It looked as if it were rotting away. I also suffered severe nose bleeds which were thick and jelly like. I felt as if I was the sole supporter of the drug industry. I now had a posh name for my flushes and rash — acute graft versus host disease. It sounded like a criminal offence, but was a result of my sister's marrow fighting my body which was alien to it.

I was now on vitamin K and cocktails to help the fevers I was having. I received one cocktail and the infusion was given over too short a time. I did my dying swan bit again. Just as suddenly as in the previous anaphalactic shock, I became dull-witted and dyspnoeic. I pressed the bell and crawled into bed. The nurse arrived after what seemed hours and told me not to get hysterical. I vowed never to utter such platitudes to my patients again. I vomited up large amounts of thick muddy brown fluid and had to be given a nebuliser. Unfortunately, my husband arrived that day and, already shocked at my poor condition, he nearly went white as he watched.

The next ordeal was my hair beginning to fall out. I was told if it fell out quickly it would regrow much better so one night I sat with my husband and shaved it all off. The giggles as the razor tickled brought the nurses and, ironically, I remembered how much my hair had cost to perm not so long ago. The dreaded graft versus host was at work. I developed rigors and my mouth condition worsened. My urine contained large amounts of bilirubin and, despite there being no evidence of damage to my cystic duct, I went even more yellow. In the mirror I saw little yellow bristles, yellow and red skin like a summer sunset, and large puffy eyes.

My children wrote regularly and sent me a little picture of how they thought I looked. My son did a full-scale poster of it and it was promptly pinned up at school. I often wondered what the other mothers thought of it. I developed a herpes infection which ate the skin around my mouth and nose, which is still scarred. I remember most how painful my mouth was. I was still receiving Vitamin K and, yes, had yet another anaphalactic reaction. This time my skin felt like a million maggots were crawling all over it. I did feel a little calmer and managed to disconnect the infusion. Large yellow patches appeared all over my body and then I collapsed. I do not remember anything else, though I was told that this had been a very serious attack.

My blood counts were rising very slowly and I was allowed to move more freely while still in the confines of the ward. The unit is totally self-contained and separate and stringent precautions are taken to prevent infections occurring. I was impatient to go home and was told that the marrow was like a little seed and must be carefully nurtured so it would grow.

I didn't tell the nurses how ill I was feeling as I wanted to go home. You'd think being a nurse I would know better. My catheter had become sloughy and my bilirubin level was well on the way to a world record. While in this state my first article was published and while re-reading about the first stage of my illness I was undergoing a second phase My bilirubin level now reached 260 umol/litre and was still rising. The infusion was discontinued and, with a promise of twice weekly out-patien appointments, I was allowed home.

The joy of my homecoming was short lived. I was rushed back to the hospital within a few days. I had acute liver failure and was feeling terrible. The cyclosporin was considered to be having an adverse effect on my liver and was discontinued. When all possibilities had been covered and I was told my husband had been sent for, the count stabilised. The bilirubin was now so high that it could no longer be registered. It was to be allowed home. I was desperate but it did help to be in my own home. I improved very slowly and made the twice weekly visits from the wilds of Lancashire down to Hammersmith. For a long time my life revolved round whether I was to go to the hospital that week or not.

Light relief came when my wig arrived. My son thought it was a dead cat. On my initial return home, my son had cuddled me then demanded to feel my little bristles and we had a good laugh at the odd way I looked. The children had given me a large poster of a woman who was starring in the current Star Trek movie. Needless to say I did not look as sexy as she.

My catheter was still in situ and was becoming a nuisance. I often caught the little cap on the end under the bath rim and the tube would stretch then release. My language was a little colourful on these occasions. I had my catheter removed on one of my visits to the hospital and it was a little reluctant and had to be yanked at forcefully.

My progress was slow but sure. My mouth did not improve much and despite many experimental drugs nothing worked. The discomfort caused eating problems. Nothing seemed to alleviate the pain and I was again feeling depressed. The sores looked awful; I could not clean my mouth and this in turn aggravated the condition. This became a major difficulty and it was a long time before it improved.

BONE MARROW TRANSPLANT
— RECOVERY

Nursing Times Magazine January 28th, 1987

MOST people consider bone marrow transplants to be the kind of operation that once done, is over and finished with. This is not true and the media's coverage of marrow transplants which claimed the recipient cured immediately is very misleading. I, like many other people, still have problems.

My main problem, initially, was my mouth. The inside was badly ulcerated and covered with large white patches. Some of the mucous membrane had thickened into tight bands which caused difficulty in opening my mouth. I also had excessive saliva and secretions and this aggravated the problem. I could not stand to clean my teeth and most oral solutions caused intense discomfort and irritation. I obtained some relief from Difflam but the effect did not last long.

I reached a good stamina level quite early on in my post-transplant period and this boosted my confidence. I had visited one lady who was still 'pottering' about the house well after a year. The visits to Hammersmith Hospital reached monthly, then two-monthly, intervals. No longer did I have to plan everything to fit in with the hospital. I still looked very odd and for the first six months my hair grew no longer than little bristles. The yellow tinge had dimmed just a little. I still had faint brown patches on my face, though these were fading.

I decided it was time that I thought about going back to work and after nine months I began the process of returning. I must admit to a feeling of trepidation about returning to work after such a long absence. I worried about what I had forgotten; would I be able to pick up the threads again? I worried about the way I looked. I worried about whether my hair would be long enough to clip to my cap.

I had been assured that going back would present no problems and that I would just report to the medical officer on my return. I was very surprised when I was told I could not continue my training. The fight against the bureaucracy to reverse the decision was just the spur I needed and my recovery was quite speedy after that.

Eventually I won and the day dawned when I returned to the hospital, absolutely terrified. The staff in the ward were marvellous and I soon felt as though I had never been away. I had to make up a year to complete my training, despite being so near finals when I left. I was carefully monitored by Hammersmith and Rossendale staff health and the only problem was the slow recovery of my mouth.

I took my final exams in October and the following six weeks waiting for the results were the worst of my life. In December, just before Christmas, I heard that I had passed. I spent a very happy Christmas and I even managed to get a job at the end of it. I was warned that if I had large amounts of time off I would be considered unfit to work but I managed to do two years with only a few days off, none directly connected to my transplant.

All was going well until I developed severe herpes zoster which was cause for some concern. It was difficult to assess just how much immunity I had against this disease. Viral infections of any sort are very dangerous to the transplant patient. I had severe pain but it did subside within three or four weeks and I returned to work with discomfort on occasions only.

I found a consultant at a nearby hospital who was prepared to take me on as he had experience of transplants with children at the Westminster Hospital, London. I was now able to have more free time as I did not have to travel to Hammersmith often on my days off. My mouth continued to improve slowly and, though there is still some thickening of the inside of my mouth, most of the ulceration has healed. I have now developed some other problems such as large, thickening patches of skin on various parts of my body, the worst on my legs.

The skin broke down and ulcerated in many places on my legs and despite careful specialist treatment, has taken nearly a year to heal. My legs are very unsightly, oedematous, and the thickening layers have caused ridging and large patches of white, dry skin. The remaining skin turned bright red and the circulation caused cramp.

I have also developed dry eye syndrome which is at the moment causing me some problems. Because of the lack of lubrication and cleaning caused by lack of tears, my eye had been ulcerating. I am now in the process of receiving treatment for this. Most of these problems result from the graft versus host disease. My body is continually being attacked by my donor's marrow. I will have problems with this for many years but as experience in dealing with these problems builds up, treatment should improve.

This rather depressing picture has not stopped me working, though I have had more time off than previously, and I am doing quite well and lead a full and active life. I have passed three 0-levels which has cheered me up considerably. I hope to be considered for a place on a conversion course, despite my school of nursing's reluctance.

I have achieved most of what I set out to do and hope my tale will encourage others to do the same. I also hoped that I have given an insight into just what is entailed in the nursing of a transplant patient and the problems which can exist long after the initial procedure. I hope that future patients will be encouraged by my progress, despite it being slow in places.

CHAPTER ONE

All Change

After Loraine hurt her back she had to retire from nursing; she and I prayed to the Lord a lot for direction. Loraine really wanted to continue to work in an area where she could help people. We felt that the Lord was directing her to manage sheltered housing where she could continue using her experience in working in the office, and nursing, so that she could carry on caring for people, especially the elderly. In 1988 Loraine joined West Pennine Housing Association as the manager of a brand-new sheltered housing complex called Brandwood in a small hamlet called Newchurch which is in the Rossendale Valley is about five miles outside Burnley. Loraine was very excited about starting this new career. We moved in just before Christmas so over Christmas and the New Year period we had the whole building to ourselves.

Loraine came up with the idea that on Christmas Day, to add some excitement for John and Carole our children, we would leave under the Christmas tree a clue which led to many other clues for them to follow all around the building to find their Christmas presents. That was one of the best Christmases that John and Carole can remember. There was one time that John was at school and the teacher was discussing with the pupils how many toilets and bathrooms they had in their home and our John said "38 toilets and 38 bathrooms". The teacher said to John "don't be silly you can't have that that many in one home" and our John insisted that he had. John was so put out about this that Loraine had to write a letter to the teacher and explain that it was sheltered housing and John was including all the toilets and bathrooms that were in the building.

In 1989 Loraine became unwell and was laid up in bed. We had the doctor out twice. The second time an elderly doctor visited who felt the back of Loraine's neck and said "she has meningitis and I'm sending her into hospital, the ambulance will be here soon" and then left. I got Loraine's things together: Loraine said "no one's carrying me down the stairs" and she got out of bed and sat on the stairs and inched her way down the stairs until she was sitting on the bottom step. Satan inflicted Loraine with meningitis and she was rushed to Burnley General Hospital where she stayed for over two weeks.

Loraine was given high doses of penicillin intravenously which caused Loraine to hallucinate. One of the hallucination moments was after Loraine had used the bedpan one night, which she gave to a male nurse and said "you want to bottle this, it's good for snakebites." Another hallucination moment was when she saw a little man painting Maori faces all over her face; Loraine said she missed the little man when he went away.

Whilst in hospital Loraine met an old lady who kept wandering off trying get a taxi or a bus home. Loraine befriended this lady and they would stand there knocking on the window to anybody who passed such as firemen or ambulance men saying "can you let me out my mummy doesn't know I'm here". Loraine and this old lady thought this was good fun, the point being that the old lady felt more comfortable with Loraine and it distracted the old lady from wandering off trying to get a taxi or a bus, which meant the staff didn't have to go chasing after her. Loraine recovered from meningitis but it left her with a bit of a memory issue and she couldn't stand strong sunlight. Two years after that, Satan inflicted her with diabetes. She had a lot of trouble controlling the diabetes with many types of insulin and got very frustrated.

In 1989 while Loraine was at West Pennine Housing Association she completed the National Wardens Certificate run by the Institute of Housing: this course included five parts - Sheltered Housing and the Role of the Warden, Understanding Ageing, The Helping Skills, The Community and Community Resources, Extended Practice based Project. She also did a one-year course in counselling.

1990 Loraine saw an advert for the Baptist Housing Association which she prayed about and felt the Lord was saying that she must apply for it. She did apply and got the job which meant we had to move to Huddersfield. At this time our daughter Carole was a resident student at an Agricultural College at Preston doing a course on "Small Animal Care". Loraine decided to have a little fun with Carole and told her that we moved but didn't tell her where and waited a few weeks before telling her where we had moved to. Carole got a bit frustrated and in the end Loraine told her that we'd moved to Huddersfield and gave her the address. All of us, including Carole, found it funny that we kept her wondering for a few weeks where we had moved to.

The Sheltered Housing Complex was run very differently than West Pennine Housing Association. Although Loraine was the manager, and had overall day-to-day running of the complex, this was overseen by a management committee from the local Baptist Church.

Loraine got on very well with the management committee who were quite involved in the social activities. They would put up the Christmas decorations and do a lunch for the residents. We went to the Baptist Church and learnt a lot about how the Baptists do things and my daughter was baptised at the Church. We met some good Christian people on that committee.

Loraine also set up a support team at the church for people in need of company or those needing food for whom she organized food parcels. Someone said "look, here come the care bears" and it wasn't complimentary, but Loraine in her usual manner turned it around and said what a good name it was, hence it becoming our official name "The Care Bears".

We also ran the Sunday school and we also went to Huddersfield Christian Fellowship for a time. Loraine and I learnt a lot while we were there about how the church can be involved in the community.

August 1992 Loraine's young sister Alison married Adam Walker. Loraine was absolutely delighted, she got her hair done and put on a lovely orangey yellow dress; she even made me wear a tie. At the wedding Loraine's mother kept coming up and asking Loraine if she was all right, she obviously thought Loraine might feel a bit hurt or jealous that all the family was at Alison's wedding when they didn't go to Loraine's wedding. Loraine didn't feel anything like that; she was delighted to be invited and enjoyed the day.

There was a sit-down meal and Loraine enjoyed meeting Adams family. As a bit of fun Loraine wrapped Adam and Alison's wedding present in newspaper and wrote all over it "*designed and wrapped by Acme packing*".

Loraine prayed about Primrose Hill Baptist Church and got a strong vision for the church and presented it in a 23 page report. I have write out three sections of this report which I feel are important for us today as when Loraine wrote them back then. They are just how Loraine wrote them.

THE PATCHWORK QUILT

I prayed one day not long after I came to Laurel Court and before I knew the people in the church or its history. I prayed to God to give me an insight into the church and for something encouraging to say to the people.

God showed me a picture of a large quilt, it was made of different squares and textures, patterns, materials and there was a glorious array of vibrant colours with different sheens and hues. The quilt was intricately sewn and each stitch was minute and so finely stitched in threads of gold and silver; I was truly amazed.

I asked God what this picture meant – He replied that the quilt was its people and church, it is to demonstrate what we should aim for and provide all that is needed such as warmth, comfort, security, protection (covering in prayer) and images and words that stimulated the imagination and most of all it is a place where to rest and to contemplate.

I thought about the quilt a lot over the next couple of days, I thought about how all the squares went together and although each was so different it made such a beauty, complete thing together. I thought how lovingly such a quilt would have been made and how much patience and diligence to fit the squares together yet use so much creativity to create such a pattern. I thought how someone different with the same squares would have perhaps created a totally different look yet all the elements were the same. This garment will certainly a garment of love. We are those squares so different with so many gifts yet we build each other up to a wonderful whole being.

Then I told God what I had seen and felt and God said there was more, look deeper, the quilt was like churches the world over, each church was so different and yet so complete together and how they achieved all that could be asked of the churches. Again the churches as a whole provided all the characteristics that we need and which God would ask of us: much later when I knew about the L.E.P this began to make sense. Different churches working together create a useful vehicle for God's work, many have different views yet we are working together.

Still I think and reflect on that quilt and the threads, of gold and silver which are salvation and redemption. I thank God for that simple picture using something we all have and understand, a simple quilt. I thank God for such a vibrant and hopeful image and then I asked "Who shall I share it with". Back came the reply-"Start with Primrose Hill Baptist"

Then I began to realise God wanted to do more with us…!!

Later I got another picture of a quilt but this quilt was a little grubby and had been ripped. The stuffing hung out of it and it seemed so neglected. The silver and gold threads had been snapped or worked loose and the squares were so faded and indistinguishable. I wept, I was filled with great sadness. A hand came into the picture and bit by bit repair of the quilt was begun. God provides all that is required for renewal, it is we who must grasp the vision and work as one under God's banner and guidance.

A FUNNY THING HAPPENED TO ME ON THE WAY TO THE FAST DAY

I felt I had different things to prepare myself about, lie down and let go and repent so that I could come with a clean heart. I take this very seriously about being ready to come before God especially when I am seeking His guidance. So often the enemy deprives us of the joy we could receive in such circumstances because he uses that little doubt or uneasiness which lies hidden in our minds.

I may not have to lay down comments about 'my way is best' or 'it's someone else's fault the church is in the state it is' or perhaps had to face up to 'past hurts and disappointment;' in fact I was feeling rather smug with myself really. Then a couple of days previously I blotted my copybook, I was very angry about something someone had done and had a fierce argument or should I say I lost my temper whilst that person remained calm. It took two days trying to avoid the issue but the morning of the fast day, and I was ready to go to church, I knew I couldn't go without doing something about it. I had to swallow my pride and apologise and mean it and it was very hard for me. I felt better after but now I have a poster on my wall that says 'Lord make my words sweet and tender for tomorrow I may have to eat them'. I was then ready to go and seek the Lord.

The day had started so well in lots of ways; firstly there was that painful apology and then I was to meet friends at the church but my son got the message wrong and I actually turned up as they left. I didn't bring any writing paper or pen and I was unable to write down the verses and prayers that people shared and I felt this was an important thing to do. I felt I would be unable to reflect as perhaps others would do on what was said as the day would be a long one with too much to remember. I find it better to write down bare facts on what is said so that I can study them at a later time.

On the first day I wasn't sure what to expect, but a fast day and prayer day had always been a joyous occasion. Instead I found a very sombre group and at first I felt very hard. My problem I knew, but I thought it might be helpful to share them with you and show you how we can often be robbed of the full blessings without realising it. I settled down and stayed till evening and this is part of what I felt God is saying to us.

I have a strong belief that it will be time of renewal for the church and that God is preparing a vision in the hearts of the people of the church and how he is giving parts to some people like a jigsaw and then to others the full picture. I know God is sharing this full picture with two others and I hope they will let me know as I feel this is will provide encouragement for them and for me.

I have shared only small parts of this vision with people and not the verses and prayers as I wish confirmation by people bringing similar if not the same words to the church independently. A feel God is setting the scene for a wonderful work in this community and I hope that you too will see as I do.

However, if you feel differently or have strong views of your own don't be afraid to share them with me, I don't believe in falling out with people who do not agree with me because I have learnt that time will prove whether a person has spoken the truth or not. Reflect carefully on what is said for it is your duty not to accept blindly the words of another person but to weigh up the words for yourself. There is enough division within our church and the wider churches without adding anything to it.

If you hear what I say and you dream as I do, if you can feel the passion I feel then come and talk to me, talk to your minister about it I am encouraged when people talk to me rather than just ignore things.

Let's be joyous, lets live as Jesus promises us, a rich and abundant life, our cups to run over.

Luke 6:38
38 Give, and it will be given to you: good measure, pressed down, shaken together, and running over will be put into your bosom. For with the same measure that you use, it will be measured back to you."
NKJV

Praise God, worship and exalt him. He is Wonderful and Mighty. He is the One who knows us individually and cares for us.

How Blessed we are.

TWO EAGLES AND A VINE (NKJV)

Ezek 17:1-24

17 And the word of the Lord came to me, saying, 2 "Son of man, pose a riddle, and speak a parable to the house of Israel, 3 and say, 'Thus says the Lord God:

"A great eagle with large wings and long pinions, Full of feathers of various colours, came to Lebanon and took from the cedar the highest branch. 4 He cropped off its topmost young twig and carried it to a land of trade; He set it in a city of merchants. 5 Then he took some of the seed of the land and planted it in a fertile field; he placed it by abundant waters and set it like a willow tree. 6 And it grew and became a spreading vine of low stature; its branches turned toward him, but its roots were under it. So it became a vine, brought forth branches, and put forth shoots.

7 "But there was another great eagle with large wings and many feathers; and behold, this vine bent its roots toward him, and stretched its branches toward him, from the garden terrace where it had been planted, that he might water it. 8 It was planted in good soil by many waters, to bring forth branches, bear fruit, and become a majestic vine."' 9 "Say,

'Thus says the Lord God:

"Will it thrive? Will he not pull up its roots, Cut off its fruit, and leave it to wither? All of its spring leaves will wither, and no great power or many people will be needed to pluck it up by its roots. 10 Behold, it is planted, Will it thrive? Will it not utterly wither when

the east wind touches it? It will wither in the garden terrace where it grew.""

11 Moreover the word of the Lord came to me, saying, 12 "Say now to the rebellious house: 'Do you not know what these things mean?' Tell them, 'Indeed the king of Babylon went to Jerusalem and took its king and princes, and led them with him to Babylon. 13 And he took the king's offspring, made a covenant with him, and put him under oath. He also took away the mighty of the land, 14 that the kingdom might be brought low and not lift itself up, but that by keeping his covenant it might stand. 15 But he rebelled against him by sending his ambassadors to Egypt, that they might give him horses and many people. Will he prosper? Will he who does such things escape? Can he break a covenant and still be delivered?

16 'As I live,' says the Lord God, 'surely in the place where the king dwells who made him king, whose oath he despised and whose covenant he broke — with him in the midst of Babylon he shall die. 17 Nor will Pharaoh with his mighty army and great company do anything in the war, when they heap up a siege mound and build a wall to cut off many persons. 18 Since he despised the oath by breaking the covenant, and in fact gave his hand and still did all these things, he shall not escape.'"

19 Therefore thus says the Lord God: "As I live, surely my oath which he despised, and my covenant which he broke, I will recompense on his own head. 20 I will spread my net over him, and he shall be taken in my snare. I will bring him to Babylon and try him there for the treason which he committed against Me. 21 All his fugitives with all his troops shall fall by the sword, and those who remain shall be scattered to every wind; and you shall know that I, the Lord, have spoken." 22 Thus says the Lord God: "I will take also one of the highest branches of the high cedar and set it out. I will crop off from the topmost of its young twigs a tender one, and will plant it on a high and prominent mountain. 23 On the mountain height of Israel I will plant it; and it will bring forth boughs, and bear fruit, and be a majestic cedar. Under it will dwell birds of every sort; in the shadow of its branches they will dwell. 24 And all the trees of the field shall know that I, the Lord, have brought down the high tree and exalted the low tree, dried up the green tree and made the dry tree flourish; I, the Lord, have spoken and have done it." NKJV

I was sitting in church on the fast day when this parable was given to me to share, which I did. I feel that God is saying that the church has done things in its own strength and that it has been rebellious. It has looked elsewhere for support or taken its eyes off God; because of this the fruit of the vine has withered and died.

Do you know if these things mean anything to you, has your church been brought low and do we need to think about such things as division gossip, lack of gifts and growth?

Look at all these areas, but not in a way to condemn people, so we can be truly sorry. Let's not look at this recalling past hurts, harsh judgements and foolishness but let's put our eyes back on the Saviour who through him all things may be possible – read what he says to us: "I myself" what hope there is in those two words, we are not abandoned but must wait for God to come himself amongst us and he will take the shoots and plant them himself.

When this is accomplished then there will be fruit and growth, we will be like a cedar tree in the area, a tree so special that it was used in the inner temple because of its look and because of its great strength and its ability to withstand all types of insect or fungal infestations.

What about verse 23 – "Under it will dwell birds of every sort; in the shadow of its branches they will dwell." Because it provides shelter, succour, shade, home, food, all necessary ingredients to a fulfilling life.

This, I believe, is the mainstay of the vision, for this speaks of different people in need from the elderly, young and homeless, mentally ill and other weaker groups in the community who will find this shelter with us, God's people, when they become a financial and a sociable liability to others in society.

What Loraine and I didn't know at the time was that the Baptist Housing Association was in negotiation with the English Churches Housing to be taken over, and this report was not going to see the light of day. It was only a matter of time before Satan ruined it all. The Baptist Housing Association was taken over by English

Churches Housing and the first thing they did was get rid of the management committee and any involvement with the church.

Loraine and I prayed about this, and God said to us "it's not what it seems, leave." We found out that English Churches Housing was secular and nothing to do with the church; it just took over small housing associations and bought up church land to build on.

Loraine left English Churches Housing and began working for Anchor Trust, one of the largest housing associations in the country, again it was a brand-new complex in Wythenshawe, Greater Manchester. Anchor Trust management knew about Loraine's illness and at that time was very supportive.

The complex had an excellent kitchen. Loraine got the Womens Royal Voluntary service involved and once a week they ran a lunch club. Right next door to the complex was a primary school and Loraine was keen to foster relationships between the elderly tenants and the pupils at the school, the first thing being getting herself on the Board of Governors. Loraine became friends with the Head of the school and the Deputy Head of the school and, before long, ladies from the flats were giving the children cookery lessons. One or two of the ladies from the flats went into the school and read to the younger children.

One day an elderly man asked Loraine about the flats. She explained about the flats and what a warden controlled accommodation was. She eventually found out that he was a widower and living in a three-bedroom house right across the road from the complex. Eventually he moved into one of the flats and we got to know him very well; his name was Tom and he was a godly man. He would write scriptures on cards and hand them out. Tom would also go into the school next door and help with the religious education lessons. Tom wrote to Loraine in 1998 saying he was still helping out at the school with reading, painting, singing and playing games.

One day Loraine got a telephone call from our son John to tell her the news that our first grandson had just been born and they have decided to call him John Christopher. Loraine's emotions got the better of her and she burst out crying; you could hear John on the other end of the telephone asking his mother what was wrong, he couldn't understand why she was crying. As John and Michelle lived in Huddersfield we had to wait a few weeks to see baby John.

About the same time Loraine's brother-in-law Adam, husband to her sister Alison, was knocked off his motorbike. He was rushed into Burnley General Hospital with very severe injuries. The consultant told Alison to prepare herself that he might not survive these injuries. This was a very testing time for Alison and with Loraine supporting and praying every night, he eventually did recover, although some permanent problems remain.

In July 1994 we finally got around to enjoying our honeymoon in Jersey during the "Battle of the Flowers". It is said it never rains during the week of the Battle of the Flowers, except the week Loraine and I went!

We chose our Hotel as the brochure advertised gourmet meals with full board; on being there we discovered that an extra charge was made for the gourmet meals! The bedroom was very small and we had to walk sideways to get around the bed. The room had a TV that received Sky but we had to watch what the manager wanted to watch. If he switched channels on Sky, then all the TVs in the hotel switched also. We therefore asked the holiday representative if we could move and she came to pick us up. I was half in the car when she set off; I am sure it was quite funny for other people to see this car moving with a man hopping along half out of the vehicle, but it wasn't funny for me at the time. We had a good time visiting Jersey Zoo and the German Underground Hospital. We obviously saw the "Battle of the Flowers" during the only time it rained. We got back to the Hotel and Loraine was so tired she fell asleep on the bed whilst speaking halfway through a word!

When we got back from our honeymoon from Jersey, Loraine decided she wanted a dog; she finally persuaded me to buy a Lhasa Apso which we called Odo from a character in the Star Trek Deep Space Nine. Loraine got a lot of pleasure from Odo; eventually he learned to get up the stairs and it was quite funny watching him come back down. Every step he jumped on, Odo sneezed and then let out a little bark. Twelve months later Loraine decided that Odo needed some company so we bought another Lhasa Apso and called her Kira also a character in the Star Trek Deep Space Nine television program. When we brought her home she was seven weeks old and we kept her in a blanket in a fruit box.

I don't think Odo was very happy when we brought Kira home; he went round the fruit box nudging the blanket with his nose until it completely buried her underneath it. Odo and Kira grew up tolerating each other; if Kira got on a cushion Odo got out; they never ever slept next to each other - they always slept separately.

Loraine felt it was time to ask her manager about the possibility of moving to a different complex. Her manager mentioned that there was a complex in Blackpool which had suffered many problems and the manager there had been dismissed for irregularities. Loraine and I decided to have a look at the complex and, after praying, Loraine was led to apply.

When we moved in, we found that there was a closed-circuit TV system in the complex and cameras on every corridor. Loraine also found the cost of cleaning supplies for the scheme was astronomical. She counselled one old lady who'd been locked in a kitchen and money had been stolen from her flat which left her traumatized. Loraine was told that's why the security cameras were installed because tenants were being robbed. The manager called the police who said "someone must have left the door open and that's how they got in."

Eventually Loraine and I started to hear the rumours of what had been going on; it was the manager herself who had been stealing and she and her husband were selling the cleaning supplies at the market. I must emphasize that these were rumours and one should not really pay attention to rumours, but it was proved factual and the manager was dismissed.

It was obvious why the Lord wanted Loraine there as the tenants needed some security, peace and reassurance that they could live their lives without worry. Loraine had to deal with some strange people in that complex - there was an old man who was very angry and violent and actually tried to hit Loraine with a telephone, and then there was a man who, if you fell out with him, would say "I am not speaking to you for twelve months" and would actually not speak to you until the twelve-month period had ended, and then start speaking to you like there had been nothing wrong.

When things settled down in the complex we decided to let Kira have a litter of pups, she had six pups and they became quite fond of Odo their dad. The pups played with Odo; they would chase him around the house and garden but he just wanted to be left alone. Loraine and I would hear his whimpering and find the pups had pursued Odo to the dining room, Odo would jump on to a chair and the pups tried to jump on the chair to play with him and he would just lie there still whimpering.

When the pups where eight weeks old we sold them, one to the daughter of one of our residents in the complex who named him Leo because he looked like a lion. When this daughter came to see her father in the complex she would bring Leo to visit. Odo and Leo became good friends and would play together; Kira would sit on the back of a chair looking down at them playing, and Kira's expression would just look like she was thinking 'what a couple of idiots'.

One day Loraine's manager gently dropped a hint that there was another problem scheme in Selby, Yorkshire. Loraine prayed about it and she felt the Lord saying "go". As it was nearer to John and our grandson we went to Selby. Also this gave us an added bonus of witnessing Selby's beautiful Abbey. The previous manager had been dismissed and as the tenants were so disillusioned with Anchor Trust they contacted their Member of Parliament to get a different housing association to manage the complex.

CHAPTER TWO

Slowing Down

Loraine worked for Anchor Trust for over nineteen years; she managed several complexes for Anchor Trust having always been sent there by God to help someone. Sometimes it was for our benefit, when the Lord wanted us to meet someone and learn something from them.

As with any large organization, Anchor's management changed; they started making their complexes non-residential for the managers and were less sympathetic toward Loraine and her illnesses; in fact Loraine's new area manager was a Muslim and knew that Loraine was a born-again Christian and he became quite difficult and nasty. Also, if Loraine was given a cheque by a resident she was encouraged by the management to tell them to make the cheque payable to Anchor instead of Anchor Trust, which made Loraine very uncomfortable as Anchor Trust was the official charity name of the Housing Association.

At the same time Loraine's illnesses were making her tired and the Lord said to her "it's time for you to slow down". Loraine asked Anchor Trust about going part-time but they were very unsympathetic, they actually saw this as an opportunity to force Loraine out of her job. Loraine and I prayed to the Lord and she asked him for a part-time complex by the sea where she could eventually retire.

She applied for a complex in St. Annes-on-Sea run by Hanover Housing; it was a part-time job, only twenty hours.

With this being a new Housing Association and the flats being leased rather than rented, Loraine had to learn a whole new way of doing things. I told her that I felt she should retire but her reply was, she felt the Lord leading her there and she had to stay busy.

There was a lady in the complex who had slight learning difficulties, was very unhappy living there and wanted to move back to Manchester where she had come from. She experienced difficulties sorting this out because the property she was in was deemed suitable by the authorities and was leasehold.

Although this was not part of Loraine's job she rose to the challenge and negotiated with the Social Services and a housing association in Manchester, and eventually she managed to get this lady moved to Manchester, which made a big difference to this lady's life. She wrote to Loraine on many occasions telling her how happy she was and how she was doing in her new home.

We started praying about which church to go to and started to ask around about different churches and what they were like. Eventually we were led to Fylde Christian Service Church where we met a couple, David and Ruth, who had a great impact on our lives. They were greeting people on the door and as soon as we entered the church Loraine turned to me and said "God sent us to meet this couple."

We had fellowship with David and Ruth in their home where we also had Bible studies and they introduced us to the teachings of Andrew Wommack which made a big difference in our lives. Off we would go to visit them every Friday, have a meal with them, followed by worship and a Bible study.

Loraine loved David and Ruth and was under no doubt that the Lord had brought us together. David is a railway enthusiast and was looking for a book that had been out of print for some time. Loraine decided that this is what she wanted to give him for Christmas, so she prayed and asked the Lord where to look, and found it on the Internet. She gave it to David for Christmas and he was surprized and extremely delighted. Loraine was always looking for ways to make people happy.

One night in April 2012 our son John was knocked down by a young woman driving on the wrong side of the road and he ended up in intensive care in Leeds. We had to drive from St Annes up the M62 to Leeds; when we got there, John was in a coma so we spoke to the consultant. He told us that John was badly injured and he may not make it. This was very distressing for Loraine and she was in floods of tears at the thought of possibly losing our son. When we got home we prayed together for healing and protection, as we knew that Satan was involved.

The next time we visited John was one of the very few jaw dropping moments we have ever had. Loraine and I both saw a seven foot tall angel at the head of John's bed with his wings unfolded around his bed like a shield. John was in a coma for about three weeks and all the time that angel never moved.

Eventually, our son John eventually was well enough to be transferred to his local hospital in Huddersfield where he lived. When he was discharged he had to struggle on crutches and a big metal frame round his right leg. Loraine and I gave thanks to the Lord that He looked after our son.

People would come up to Loraine and me and ask how we could be so relaxed after what had happened to our son. Our reply was: "we know that the Lord sent an angel to watch over John." Some people understood; some people didn't.

As Loraine was beginning to feel tired she thought it was time to retire so we started to look for property to rent and, in preparation, told her employer she wanted to go non-residential, in other words live away from the complex.

CHAPTER THREE

The Journey Home – To The Lord

Even though I know this is going to be the hardest chapter to write, as it will be like re-living it all over again, I feel it has to be told.

In July 2013 Loraine was told by Blackpool Victoria Hospital that she had liver cancer and it was too advanced to treat. We asked our family doctor to refer Loraine to The Christie at Manchester. Christie thought Loraine might be eligible to go on drugs that wouldn't cure the cancer but would stop it from spreading any further, but by the time Blackpool Victoria Hospital sent Loraine's scans and notes to The Christie at Manchester, Loraine was not eligible for the treatment.

Loraine and I prayed a lot and we put ourselves in the hands of the Lord. She said the Lord had spoken to her and told her that she was going to have total healing. When we prayed we kept getting Luke 8:43 about the woman who came from behind and touched the border of Jesus' garment. We both felt it was telling us to forget the doctors, nurses and the councillors and focus totally on Jesus.

Shortly after that, Loraine got up one morning and said to me "the Lord sent me an angel". I asked what he looked like and she said "he looked like a man all in white and wearing a corduroy jacket; he was leading her through the crowds reading passages from the Bible".

We also went to Andrew Wommack's Charis Bible College in Dewsbury, West Yorkshire for prayer, stayed overnight in Huddersfield to see our son John and grandsons, and went once more to Dewsbury on 6th November when they opened their Healing School.

Eventually we got a two bedroomed house and I started moving in some of our belongings. At that time Loraine was taken ill again and ended up back in hospital where she grew worse, she could barely walk and wasn't eating properly.

One day the consultant came in to talk to us and said to Loraine and me "we are no longer talking months but weeks and we should prepare ourselves", at that point she was tearful, and cried out "Lord you promised me." I settled Loraine down and told her to trust in the Lord. A couple of days later when I visited Loraine, she told me she had a visit from Jesus who took hold of her arms and said to her "get up Loraine", which she did. She then asked Jesus "why are you doing this to me?" His reply was "because I love you." That day she managed to walk to the toilets by herself and she had a little more to eat. She also said that she told Jesus she was sorry she was going to miss his birthday. I asked her what she meant by this but she brushed it off and said it doesn't really matter.

The hospital decided to send Loraine home and by this time I had most of the furniture moved from the old flat down to the new house. Loraine would not be able to get up the stairs so we made her bed downstairs in the living room. By the time Loraine came home from hospital everything was set up for her and the district nurses were coming in twice a week. I had morphine in the fridge in case she needed it, and she had carers coming in twice a day to get her up and help put her back to bed.

By this time Loraine was growing tired; she would sleep most of the day and night and I was sleeping in a reclining chair next to the bed in case she needed anything. She was not eating properly so we got her some milky food supplements.

I got a pack of CDs free from Andrew Wommack Ministries. One of them was Healing Scriptures which Loraine liked and she would fall asleep listening to them.

One day Loraine said the Angel with the corduroy jacket was back and was crying out exaltations. On 28th November Loraine told me she had seen a new angel attired in bright autumn colours trimmed with gold. I told her to get hold of him because he might have her healing; obviously it is only by the Spirit you can see angels.

On 29th of November at three o'clock in the morning Loraine woke me up and said her stomach felt heavy. I turned on the light as Loraine said she was going to be sick, I grabbed the bowl and Loraine vomited blood and I said "this is not good." I therefore rang for an ambulance and Loraine was taken into Blackpool Victoria Hospital, she was treated in casualty and I was told it was looking serious so I telephoned her sister Alison at about four o'clock in the morning. I left a message on her answering machine and rang our son John and told him he should come over from Huddersfield. When Alison arrived I told her that Loraine was dying. I broke my heart; Alison put her arms round me, and I cried on her shoulder; I did not know what to do. When John arrived I told him what was going on and he told me to ring Carole our daughter which I did, telling her to come to the hospital. Alexander, Loraine's brother, and his partner Christine then turned up and they were very upset.

The last word I heard Loraine say was "that went well". I could leave that as it is and it would be a poignant word on her life, but actually the fact is she was pulling on bed rails trying to make herself comfortable and she didn't have the strength to do it. After saying those words she went back to sleep and didn't wake up again.

Eventually she was transferred to Acute Medical where we all headed. We met Carole and John our son and daughter, John's partner Helen, Alexander and Christine his wife, Alison, Loraine's sister and her husband Adam. Eventually Adam went to inform Loraine's mum and dad. I asked a member of staff if a minister could come and pray with Loraine, and eventually one turned up, prayed a passage from the Bible then ticked his box and went.

By this time, I was getting so distressed I telephoned David and Ruth to come right away and pray with Loraine. They prayed with Loraine for some time but Loraine did not know they were there; she was breathing heavily and fast asleep and to be quite honest I think her spirit was already leaving her body at that time.

David and Ruth stayed until nine thirty, took time to meet the family and eventually left. We all stayed with Loraine and she went home to be with the Lord at about 10 o'clock that night on 29th November, with her family around her except for Carole who had gone to my house to see to the dog. I think Loraine would have liked to have gone home to the Lord from home with the family around her.

Everyone left the hospital and came to my house. Alexander brought me back home in my car. I had to tell Carole that her mother had died and we both cried on each other's shoulder. Everyone stayed for a while, had a hot drink and then went home. John and Helen stayed in a hotel in Blackpool and Carole stayed with me in the house.

I registered Loraine's death on 1st December and then came all the relevant paperwork notifying the appropriate people about the death. Every time I filled in one form I got two back and it seemed never ending.

I went round to David and Ruth's house and cried on Ruth's shoulder for what seemed a very long time. Eventually I explained why I had come. I wanted David and Ruth to officiate at Loraine's funeral. Loraine did not want a minister taking the funeral who did not know her, she wanted somebody who knew her and had a belief in the Lord like she did.

Loraine's funeral was on 13th December 2013. David and Ruth led the funeral and produced all the service sheets. It was a beautiful service. As we entered the building the song playing was "In the Garden" and the hymn during the service was "Amazing Grace" the original words by John Newton. As everybody was leaving, the song "Bridge over Troubled Water" recorded by Simon and Garfunkel was playing, which was one of Loraine's favourite songs.

WHAT JUST HAPPENED? That was the question I was asking myself when I was alone. Over forty one years of marriage had just ended; the future we had planned was torn up into small tatters. I was wrestling with this, and every part of our lives was playing out in my head.

I was depressed and couldn't sleep, and every time I went to take my medication a voice in my head said "take them all and you can be with her". My doctor prescribed for me antidepressants and sleeping pills, and referred me to the Mental Health Clinic for counselling.

I was also wrestling with the fact that the Lord seemed to have changed His mind as He promised a total healing yet Loraine had gone home to the Lord. I felt that the best part of me had been ripped away, everything we had planned for the future had gone, it says in:

Matt 19:5
Be joined to his wife, and the two shall become one flesh' NKJV.

That was Loraine and me; we always did everything together. I was so empty inside I would pray to the Lord to take me home so that I could be with Him and Loraine. I became frightened of the future. I did not want to be a lonely old man who went around the family because he had nothing better to do. I don't know how I would have got through this traumatic time in my life without my family and David and Ruth.

One night when I was in bed and I had finished praying, the Lord told me the reason he had taken Loraine home. This is what He told me "her spirit was faithful and strong but Satan had plagued her virtually all her life and she was tired, and she felt that she could no longer fight another bout of cancer; she had no fear of death and she knew what was waiting for her when she arrived in heaven. One day I would join her in heaven and He still has work for us to do together".

To try to verify what the Lord had said, I looked back at everything including the visitation of the Angel that Loraine had seen, wondering if we had got it wrong.

All sicknesses come from Satan and he certainly plagued Loraine with sickness. She had leukaemia for which she had a bone marrow transplant in the eighties, from that she got "graft vs host" disease which left her scarred from the radiation and her tear ducts were destroyed because of it.

Then she got meningitis which left her with photophobia, then she got diabetes, after that her knees started crumbling away and she needed new knees. Later polyps developed in her stomach which were surgically removed at the hospital. Next, a small tumour appeared on her kidney and a larger tumour on her liver. Satan had certainly plagued Loraine.

Loraine said she had been given an angel wearing a corduroy jacket who was leading her through the crowds reading scriptures and introducing her. We both assumed he was leading her through the crowd to get to Jesus and touch Him.

The Lord allowed Loraine to go home because that's what she wanted. She was tired of fighting and wanted some peace. This angel could only be announcing Loraine's imminent arrival in heaven, not guiding her through the crowds.

Looking back when the consultant in the hospital told Loraine that it was a matter of weeks not months, Loraine cried and said "Lord you promised". I believe that was the time when the Lord gave Loraine the choice of going home with Him or stay here. Loraine knew what was waiting for her in heaven because of other experiences in Hammersmith during the bone marrow transplant.

Our children are grown up, in their thirties and forties and our grandchildren are in their teens and early twenties. Also, I was by this time secure in our new home. I don't think Loraine wanted to fight anymore and decided to go home to the Lord where we will all eventually be. Loraine didn't tell me all this because she wouldn't want to hurt me and knew that I would be reunited with her one day.

Less than twenty four hours before Loraine went home to the Lord, Loraine said the Angel in the corduroy jacket had returned and he was doing exaltations. She also said there was a seven foot angel in beautiful autumn colours and gold.

When she saw these Angels, and when she saw Jesus, I told her to grab hold of them because they could have her healing, but I believe Loraine knew that this angel had come to take her home to the Lord.

People may say Loraine was hallucinating because of the drugs but Loraine didn't take any; she only took insulin for the diabetes. Yes, I had morphine in the fridge but Loraine never took any, the Lord took her home before she had any pain.

CHAPTER FOUR

But what about me, John Gibson

But what about me, John Gibson, the husband left behind: I was in emotional pain and a wreck. Simeon said to Mary, mother of Jesus *Luke 2:35 (yes, a sword will pierce through your own soul also) NKJV.* I have an idea of what she must have gone through watching Jesus on the cross.

I could easily have blamed the Lord for taking away Loraine and leaving me like this. I received two confirmations. The first confirmation happened after Christmas 2013, when the Lord told me that I should go to Lytham Christian Centre. The first visit I was in the middle of worshipping when this old man came in and blurted out that morning God spoke to him. He had been brought to the church from the dementia ward by the nurses, the elders of the church took him out and made him a cup of tea. I wanted to hear what he had to say so I sat facing him and said "what did the Lord say to you?" He told me his life story and when he got up to date I repeated the question, "what did the Lord say to you?". He replied that the Lord said his wife is happy in heaven. I asked him "how long is it since your wife went to the Lord?" He said seven years.

This is just what Loraine would have done, sent an elderly person. I believe in his confused mind he thought the message was for him but the message was for me, as I truly believed the Lord sent me to that church on that very day. Whether you believe that's right or wrong, it still comforts me.

The second confirmation was at Lytham Christian Centre; a lady out of the worship team saw a picture of a woman holding on to the cross. When I reflect on what I told Loraine when Jesus appeared, which was to get hold of him and not let go, it made me smile hearing about that picture. I then imagined Loraine holding on to Jesus and Him saying "get off me you silly woman" and Loraine not letting him go.

I made a commitment before Loraine died that I would do the Correspondence Bible Course from Andrew Wommack's Charis Bible College, I also committed to finishing Loraine's book as I believe that Loraine knew she wouldn't finish it and that someone else would have to complete it. Loraine chose the title "The Journey Home – Daughter", I believe that title meant the journey home to the Lord.

I also made a commitment to look after Kira until she died, Odo had died a few years earlier. Four months after Loraine had passed on, Kira died from heart failure; she was nineteen years old. That brought back all the memories and I was terribly upset and heartbroken. That night I was lying in bed upset when Loraine's face appeared right in front of me and smacked a big kiss right on my lips, and I actually felt her lips against mine. There weren't any words said, and then she just disappeared as quickly as she appeared.

At every opportunity, Satan still plagues me. I do resist him as much as I can but he keeps coming back. The Lord told me to watch over Loraine but at night time I struggle to sleep and Satan keeps putting it in my head, did I smother her by watching over her too much, was there anything more I could do, did I fail Loraine in any way, did she really love me; was she happy? I find it hard to get to sleep with all this running around my head. I stopped taking the sleeping pills but up to this point I'm still taking the antidepressants. I wake up in the morning and forget for a few seconds that Loraine is no longer with me.

Six-months have passed since Loraine went to be with the Lord; I feel frightened of what is to come and what to do from this point on. When I have finished what I committed myself to do, I wonder what I will do with the rest of my life. I pray to the Lord for direction in my life but at this point I have not received any answer; perhaps the answer will come after I finish what I committed myself to do.

People are saying to me "get a hobby, it will take your mind off it, it will give you something to occupy yourself, or, it's the grieving process like there's a box out there and people who lose someone are put in a box called the grieving process. What nonsense, everybody deals with grief in their own way. You can love someone very deeply like I did with Loraine; the pain of losing them is always there but it changes and you learn to deal with it, it's a different kind of pain but it's still there and always will be.

It has been 12 months since Loraine went home to be with the Lord and I can tell you that the answer from the Lord came about my future. When I finished the correspondence course from Andrew Wommack Charis Bible College the Lord told me to do the second year at the college which surprised me very much because the second year is not a correspondence course. I would have to attend the Charis Bible College Yorkshire. If anybody had told me a few years ago to go back to college I would have thought they were crazy with all my problems, imagine going back to college at my age! But that's exactly what I've done and it's been the best thing I have ever done apart from marrying Loraine.

The college staff and pupils have been very supportive, after they prayed, the dyslexia has gone, I've been cured. Because the dyslexia has gone, I have been buying books and computer programmes to improve myself. I've even given a lesson to the first year students out of the Discipleship Evangelism book, and given a short talk to my class which has taken me right out of my comfort zone. I was such an introvert that if anybody had told me what I would be doing now, they would have needed binoculars to see me running the other way.

I talk about Loraine all the time at college; they must be tired of hearing me but I miss her so much and I want to get across to them just what she was like, my whole life with Loraine seems to have been directing me to this point of my life where I am now. I wish Loraine was here with me enjoying this moment but she is joyous being with the Lord and am sure she is proud of what I am doing, and I can sense that she is with me and supporting me in everything I do.

It is now 1ˢᵗ April 2015. I have just got back from a week's mission trip to Bulgaria, I stayed in the town called Kyustendil. We travelled to many towns and villages. These included Dupnitsa, Popoviyane, Trun, Pernik and Sofia capital of Bulgaria. We saw many people healed, brought to the Lord and baptised in the Holy Spirit. I can honestly say that I have never experienced anything like that in my life.

Loraine once got a picture of me being out on a mission field; it was so strong a picture I even got myself a passport but it was never used and that was many years ago. On the mission trip after I was ministered to by Chance *I just had a good cry*. Chance ministered to me in truth and honesty. He said I have to let Loraine go; if I didn't it would eat me inside and affect how I did my ministry and not for the better. I thought I had. Obviously I haven't, as just another good cry followed and I wept like a baby. I am going to have to pray and get ministered to again. I have to let Loraine go as it was she who went home to the Lord. I didn't, because the Lord has work for me to do. I graduate from the Charis Bible College in 2015 and received my Certificate at the Grace and Faith Conference in Telford in May. I have finished all the commitments that I made and then it will be *all change* for me. I have to put my life in the hands of the Lord and He will guide me in the work he wants me to do.

People ask me why I would want to do the second part of this book. The answer is simple, I feel it's important that you know how Loraine continued her walk with God and demonstrate that contrary to what the secular world would have you believe, God still has a plan for us all. The biggest lie that Satan would like you to believe is that he and God do not exist, but God does exist. All you need to do is have faith and believe. Faith is believing without the evidence of seeing. To give a <u>basic</u> example of this, I know that Fort Knox exist

I believe it has a lot of gold in it but I've never seen it, I've never even been to America but I have the faith that the gold is in Fort Knox.

When I did the Charis Bible College course we had to go on a mission trip I went to Bulgaria were I saw God do miraculous works. God is as relevant today as he always has been. There are many religions out there that tell you that healing and the gifts of the spirit are not for today, that they have passed; that is utter rubbish. Look at the following two Bible verses.

Matt 28:19-20
19 Go therefore and make disciples of all the nations, baptizing them in the name of the Father and of the Son and of the Holy Spirit, 20 teaching them to observe all things that I have commanded you; and lo, I am with you always, even to the end of the age." Amen.
NKJV

John 14:12-14
12 "Most assuredly, I say to you, he who believes in Me, the works that I do he will do also; and greater works than these he will do, because I go to My Father. 13 And whatever you ask in My name, that I will do, that the Father may be glorified in the Son.
NKJV

If you accept Jesus as your Saviour and invite him into your life and have faith that Jesus can work through you, **he will work through you** and this is because as it says in John 14:12 *"because I go to My Father"* I know that God exists I have to talked to God and he has talked to me.

John 10:27-29
27 My sheep hear My voice, and I know them, and they follow Me. 28 And I give them eternal life, and they shall never perish; neither shall anyone snatch them out of My hand.
NKJV

Loraine and I looked back at our lives and saw God's hand in it, God has a plan for us all but we have free will which means we do not have to follow God's plan but if you give your life to Jesus and follow God's plan you will prosper and have life in abundance.

When Loraine went home to be with the Lord I fell apart, but God had a plan to get me through If I had not come into agreement with God's plan I doubt whether I would be here but I did agree with God's plan and he guided me through the dark times to where I am today.

Loraine and I received a lot of good advice, don't get married too early, don't have your children too early, don't have the bone marrow transplants have chemotherapy. However, we did listen to God, but if we had listened to all the so called good advice we would not have any children or grandchildren because the chemotherapy would have made that impossible, If Loraine had not received the bone marrow transplants which was very experimental back in the early eighties she would have gone to the Lord then, as chemotherapy for leukaemia was not very successful.

So I wrote the second part of this book because I knew that's what Loraine wanted to show how she carried on walking with the Lord. and to show that God is as relevant today as he has always been and we can still walk with the gifts of the Holy Spirit. And I know all this from personal experience with my own walk with the Lord.

I am reminded of a quote from Joan of Arc *"If I were to say God sent me, I shall be condemned, but God really did send me."* This could be a prophecy for today for if you say God sent you then you're condemned as a fool, but God did send me, so if I am a fool, I am a fool for God.

CHAPTER FIVE

So Who Was Loraine?

Loraine Rachel Perry was born 14th of May 1955, brought up in a little town called Shawforth, a suburban village within the Rossendale borough of Lancashire and married John Robert Gibson on 29th of July 1972. Well that's that out of the way.

When I met Loraine she had problems, but didn't we all in our teenage years? We did, however, know that we loved each other, and that God brought us together, so despite all the good advice and the problems we had, and against Loraine's parents' wishes, we did get married. None of Loraine's family came to the wedding; they boycotted it, which I know hurt Loraine deeply. The relationship between Loraine and both her parents did improve, but she felt she could not go to her relatives homes without being invited. Could it be because of the way she was treated or how she was brought up, I cannot say? We had our dogs groomed at Nelson so that Loraine could say to her mother and father "I'm bringing the dogs over to be groomed, is it okay if we pop-in?" Loraine's sister Alison very rarely invited us over so Loraine did not get to see Lauren and Jacob her niece and nephew whom she loved, as much as she wanted. I do not believe there was any malice on anybody's part; I think it was just how Loraine was.

As things improved with Loraine's mother and father, I asked her "is all forgiven now?" Loraine just turned around, raised an eyebrow and said "there is nothing to forgive, they're my mother and father, just put it all behind you and move on;" she was right. Loraine loved her mother and father and she saw nothing to forgive no matter how much they hurt her. I felt I was tolerated by Loraine's parents because I was her husband. Loraine's family showed me kindness but there was *that atmosphere*. The only time I did not feel that atmosphere was when we visited Loraine's brother Alexander and his wife Christine; I could be totally wrong but it is how I felt.

Enough of all that. "Who was Loraine?" Loraine grew and matured and became the kindest person you could ever meet. She could not see the bad in anybody, she could only see the good. In all the years I was married to Loraine I never heard her say a bad thing about anybody. If you needed anything and Loraine had it then it was yours. As Loraine was the manager of a sheltered housing complex she would often volunteer me to do jobs for the tenants without asking me; the tenants would come up to me and say "I believe you're going to tune in my TV" or "I believe you're going to screw that cupboard back to the wall for me", and I wouldn't know anything about this. Loraine's love for people and she always wanting to do the right thing for them and help them that meant that she often was taken advantage of, but when I pointed out that fact to her, she would say "well we were helping people and it doesn't matter".

The Lord said to Loraine many years ago when she was having her bone marrow transplant "You have been blessed with peace and people you touch can receive that same blessing, go and do the work I have for you". This was certainly true. I have seen Loraine sit down on a park bench next to a complete stranger, and by the time that stranger left they had told Loraine all their problems and all their life story. When they got up to go they said to Loraine "it was lovely talking to you, I feel a lot better and my worries seem to have gone." This is what it was like; wherever Loraine went, people just seemed to feel the peace within her.

Loraine was always listening to what God wanted her to do whether this was applying for a new complex that meant us moving, or send someone a word of encouragement or to donate money anonymously. The Lord would often give Loraine a picture and a word for someone; she would paint the picture, print the words on it that God gave her, and frame it to pass on to that person.

Loraine had a deep relationship with the Lord; she would write prayers on cards and place them in little envelopes. She would write letters to the Lord like she was writing to a best friend or family; she would put in the letters how she felt whatever worries she had, what she was looking forward to and just general chitchat. Loraine knew instinctively just how easy it was to become a Christian.

Matt 11:28-30
28 Come to Me, all you who labor and are heavy laden, and I will give you rest. 29 Take My yoke upon you and learn from Me, for I am gentle and lowly in heart, and you will find rest for your souls. 30 For My yoke is easy and My burden is light."
NKJV

Romans 10:9 & 10 According to this scripture "When you confess with your mouth the Lord Jesus, and believe in your heart that God raised him from the dead, you shall be saved". For with the heart one believes unto righteousness, and with the mouth confession is made unto salvation.
NKJV

This means that you are actually "born again" as mentioned in John 3:3. Jesus then becomes your Lord and Saviour and we believe that He went to the cross, bore all our infirmities and diseases, and forgave all our sins (by becoming sin himself), past, present, and future and reconciles us to God. This is the one that many people have the most trouble with, in the same way Nicodemus did in the Bible.

John 3:1-8
3 There was a man of the Pharisees named Nicodemus, a ruler of the Jews. 2 This man came to Jesus by night and said to Him,

"Rabbi, we know that You are a teacher come from God; for no one can do these signs that You do unless God is with him."

3 Jesus answered and said to him, "Most assuredly, I say to you, unless one is born again, he cannot see the kingdom of God."

4 Nicodemus said to Him, "How can a man be born when he is old? Can he enter a second time into his mother's womb and be born?"

5 Jesus answered, "Most assuredly, I say to you, unless one is born of water and the Spirit, he cannot enter the kingdom of God. 6 That which is born of the flesh is flesh, and that which is born of the Spirit is spirit. 7 Do not marvel that I said to you, 'You must be born again.' 8 The wind blows where it wishes, and you hear the sound of it, but cannot tell where it comes from and where it goes. So is everyone who is born of the Spirit."
NKJV

Baptism in Water is quite straightforward as a sign of repentance. To receive the Baptism in the Holy Spirit is when you invite Him to come into you and you will know when He does. The benefits of receiving the Holy Spirit will come to you as you grow in faith and you study the Bible.

Then the revelation of the two Commandments that Jesus gave us becomes clear. If you can obey these two commandments then you will be obeying the Ten Commandments Moses gave us, because if you love your neighbour as yourself you wouldn't want to steal from him or commit adultery with his wife or murder him.

Matt 22:37-40
37 Jesus said to him, "'You shall love the Lord your God with all your heart, with all your soul, and with all your mind.' 38 This is the first and great commandment.

39 And the second is like it: 'You shall love your neighbour as yourself.' 40 On these two commandments hang all the Law and the Prophets." NKJV

Notice that the two Commandments involve love. Love is a spiritual gift from God always revolving around a relationship. These two Commandments are very important as they speak of a relationship. Commandment one talks about loving God with all your heart, soul and mind. This is saying that the Lord wants a personal loving relationship with you.

The second commandment is saying virtually the same, having a loving relationship with your neighbour as you would want them to have a loving relationship with you.

Loraine never broke these Commandments. It is a shame that the rest of the world cannot obey these two Commandments; if they did, what a better world we would live in. Loraine would say "when I die if how I lived made a difference to just one person I can die happy". Loraine made a difference to hundreds of people, so I am absolutely confident that she died happy.

Now for the controversial bit it is said there are people on this earth whom the Lord has given souls of angels but they don't know they have souls of angels. The Lord sends them to find out how people deal with other people who show them nothing but kindness and goodness and generosity, and to find whether greed and selfishness is prevalent in the world.

If this is true, then Loraine had a soul of an angel. That would explain why Satan plagued her all her life, and how the Lord brought her back home. You as the reader may not believe this but it gives me comfort to believe this and I do believe this. To those people who ever met Loraine and she showed you love and kindness, did you show love and kindness back?

Hebrews 13:2
Do not forget to entertain strangers, for by so doing some have unwittingly entertained angels.
NKJV

You could say yes but you're Loraine's husband and you're seeing everything through rose-coloured glasses. You're right, I am Loraine's husband and I love her very deeply. There is a saying - "just because someone's paranoid doesn't mean that there is nobody after them". Just because I'm wearing rose-coloured glasses doesn't mean that what I see is not correct, and we should all be taking notice of Hebrews 13:2

Loraine had a favourite saying "if it matters to me then it matters to the Lord" and she turned round and put it in reverse "if it matters to the Lord it should matter to me". I think we should all keep those sayings in our mind. Loraine left me a note (I don't know when she intended me to find it) which said *"When my time comes to leave the world it is your face I want to kiss goodbye. It's your hand I want to hold as I slip into eternity. I want to look into your eyes and see I mattered, not how I look or how much money I made or how talented I was. I want to look into the eyes of someone who loved me and see I mattered."* Loraine also left me four quotes from the Bible, 1 Samuel 27:31, Matthew 28:11-20, Psalm 63, Proverbs 22:7-23. Loraine went home to be with the Lord.

Her leaving me nearly destroyed my life. That life came to an end. Now I am waiting for the Lord to guide me into a new life, to guide me into what He wants me to do.

Loraine will always be in my thoughts and my heart. The gift of peace the Lord gave Loraine was a different sort of peace than we understand - it was a deep peace, a peace that only comes through love and understanding and caring not just for one person but all the people.

Looking back on both our lives together it shows that the Lord will not abandon any of us. He deals with you where your faith is. I am however going to end this book with Loraine's words:

"That went well"

Lightning Source UK Ltd.
Milton Keynes UK
UKOW02f1614161016

285402UK00001B/85/P